Christianity

Johann Baptist Krebs

Christianity

or
God and Nature Only One
Through the Word

Johann Baptist Krebs

translated by Kerry A Nitz

K A Nitz
AUCKLAND, NEW ZEALAND

Christenthum
published in German 1844
under the pseudonym J. B. Kerning

This translation into New Zealand English
Copyright © K A Nitz 2023
All rights reserved

ISBN: 978-0-473-69214-8

Table of Contents

Translator's Note 7
Foreword 9
Introduction 11
The Parable 15
The Visit 19
The Second Visit 25
The Alliance of Friendship 35
Fragments 41
A New Acquaintance 45
The Third Parable 51
The Relative 57
Visit to the Doctor 61
Prophecy 65
The Rural Excursion 71
The Bible 81
Wisdom 85
The Liaison 91
The Self Perspective 99
The Contest 103
The Correspondence 109
    Deacon to the Doctor 109
    The Doctor to the Deacon 111
    Deacon to the Doctor 112
    The Doctor to the Deacon 113
    Deacon to the Doctor 121
    Doctor to the Deacon 123
Of the Doctor's Return 127
The Simplest Dogma 131
The Cataract 139
First Attack 147
Orthodoxy 149
Reconciliation 155
About the Author 167

Translator's Note

For the English translation of Bible texts I have made use of the King James Version. Where I thought it would be helpful I have also inserted missing Biblical citations in the footnotes.

The author's somewhat idiosyncratic approach to presenting dialogue has also been retained.

The names of the characters may be worth thinking about for their connotations:

Doctor Wehrmann:	*Wehrmann* is a term for soldier, but also for fireman.
Assessor Selbach:	*Sel.* is a common abbreviations for *selig*, meaning blessed or blissful. *Bach* is a term for a stream or brook.
Deacon Wohlfart:	*Wohlfahrt* means welfare.
Professor Solbring:	*Sol* is a term for brine, salt water; and *bring* is the singular imperative of *bringen*, meaning to bring.
Dean Blumhof:	Flower garden.
Parson Punter:	(No obvious German meaning, though *bunter* means more colourful or more confused.)
Physician Borndach:	*Born* is a term for well or spring; *Dach* is a roof — so roof over a well.
Parson Gutmann:	Good man (or possibly man of the manor).
Parson Pfriener:	(No obvious German meaning, though possibly related to *Pfründe*, meaning benefice, or *Pfriemer*, user of an auger.)

Foreword

Anyone who sees the title of this work will wonder about the expression — Christianity — and think it must refer to *the* Christianity. — The author was initially also of this view; but when he started drafting it, the Christianity stood so universal, so great and comprehensive before him, that it seemed sufficient to him to limit himself in his views and to say: what I am capable of expressing is certainly Christianity, but not the Christianity in its immeasurable dignity and significance.

Having said this, the reader will not resent the author for not getting drawn into the entire symbolism of the life of Christ and merely choosing individual points of light from it in order to comprehend it in the greatest possible purity and to present it to the Christian public. These points of light, however, are precisely those which in other religious writings are most rarely touched on and grappled with. It is therefore to be foreseen that the newness of a few ideas must surprise to begin with, but by closer examination must certainly be found to be genuine because these ideas agree with the vein of the Bible, and nothing is contained in it which would be contrary to the canonical laws of the apostle and the prophets upon which Christianity rests. For this reason the author hands over these pages in good spirits to the public in that he foresees that it will appear to some, as to him, that they feel joy when they can say to themselves: that which I have, even if it is not the Christianity in its infinite fullness, is though — Christianity, which qualifies me to penetrate into the temple of the all-encompassing universality from which the Christian Church has drawn its teachings.

Those born from dust must seek the universality from the particulars. In this way they obtain a certainty where they can say to themselves: the points of light which I now see are the lights of heaven which can lead me to the brilliantly radiant residence of those proven ones who achieve in the spirit of our sublime religion the goal of their existence. Truth, God, and eternity are the goals of humanity, hence each should struggle and strive so that they will someday bear testimony to not having lived in vain. To this end the author hands over the following to the public and abandons himself to the happy hope of not being misunderstood by impartial readers.

***

Introduction

Ask, and it shall be given you; seek, and ye shall find; knock, and it shall be opened unto you:

For every one that asketh receiveth; and he that seeketh findeth; and to him that knocketh it shall be opened.*

On these two verses rests the test and the practise of Christianity; for in order to receive, you must learn to ask; in order to find, learn to seek, and so that it is opened to us, learn to knock.

The knocking must refer to a technical activity; for it seems too much is asked of the healthy human mind to want to make it believe it is only spoken in the way of an analogy, and that you could knock with thoughts and feelings, or even with prayer. — In the first times of Christianity the confessors struck themselves in order to awaken the spirit, often with the palm of the hand, often even with the fist to the chest and let it, when the spirit was aroused, lie a long time on it in order to feel its influence all the longer and more certainly. The Jews, when they had offended the Lord and were in distress, struck themselves on the hips in order to reconcile themselves with Him again all the sooner.

In seeking, two things are to be taken into account: firstly *where*, and secondly *what* we seek. — If we knew the spirit of Christianity, we would not for a moment be in any doubt here. But we must, even if not now, but in the following, make the attempt to enlighten the reader over it.

The request seems to enclose a formal art in itself, if it should prove that anyone who then asks is given. — What sort of art would that be? — How is it to be learnt?

The person asks. To them it is given. — But who gives? — Answer: God. As soon as anyone who then asks is given, God, the giver, is no longer free, but forced to the giving.

How could that be? — Can the giver be forced to the giving? — And who forces them? — Perhaps the request? — Then

---

* [Tr.: Matthew 7:7–8.]

the giver would be bound to the request and dispenses with all freedom. The requestor, however, would have complete power, in so far as the giver were dependent on the request.

According to the ways of humanity, we consider a request to not be resting on any legal basis where the giver, with all fairness to the request, can grant or refuse. In this category the giver is free; the requestor, however, is at the mercy of an aimless arbitrariness.

The person requests; God grants. — God is unconditionally free, for in Him is power and wisdom. The person, however, must also be free, if he shall portray a true image of God.

The human is free, and his natural nobility consists of that. But God cannot be any less free, otherwise He forgoes His fatherhood and power, and the creation stands above him.

The creation above the creator! — The instrument over the maker! — How are these views to be united with the nature of God and the freedom of humanity without hitting too close to the former or latter?

The human is free; for as he asks, he will receive; but God, the eternal giver, has poured out His gifts, that is, His spirit, into the creation and made a point of attraction for them in the interior of the human in which the radiance of the creator collects and binds the creation most closely with Him. As a result God in his infinite goodness has given everything in advance, and the human need only make himself skilled at turning himself with his request towards these divine gifts that are already given in advance and thereby asserting his right of possession.

We must learn to ask, but not only with the mouth, rather also in the spirit and in the truth, then we will certainly be given. — We must be able to draw from the eternal sea of life which flows around us, in us, and into all regions, then we will be the masters of existence and look, since our share is inexhaustible, towards ever newer gifts.

These treasures express nothing else but those Biblical verses — ask, and it shall be given you, etc. — Provided that the two verses have canonical truth in themselves, the given sentences are also true, and the human possesses a freedom over which he is not only amazed, filled with thanks, but which he can seldom entirely comprehend. — In the art of

Introduction

asking, seeking, and knocking lies hidden the great secret of humanity, and we have nothing to do but learn and practise this art in order to make our lives into a paradise.

***

The Parable

In the capital of Z...t there lived a Doctor Wehrmann, who dedicated himself with zeal from his youth onwards to the sciences, studied theology at the university, and had obtained his doctorate. He also possessed, next to his penchant for philosophical studies, a special preference for the plastic arts, in whose criticism he had advanced so far as to be in a position when examining a work of art to feel the degree of enthusiasm in which the artist found himself when he was making it. This gave him cause to treat theology, principally Christianity, also as an art which, like every other art, had its scientific foundation, but in its practice was purely productive. — After completing his studies, a significant inheritance fell to him through the death of an uncle, at which he decided to live as a private individual in order to be able to satisfy his thirst for knowledge unhindered. Through untiring, but uninhibited research, he obtained in respect to religion and philosophy, which were not to be separated in his mind, such an assuredness of judgement that to him things which to others were still tightly locked puzzles became as clear as the bright light of day. — In this way he lived amongst the residents of the capital, in part unappreciated, but in part also honoured as a man who possessed the courage and ability to show the source of truth to anyone who strove for it. — He had made it his duty also to speak everywhere that opportunity offered about higher truths in order to lead, if not the masses, then here and there an individual from the darkness to the light.

One evening he found himself at the house of the senior civil servant Weller, where a party of honest men had gathered for an evening banquet which was being given in commemoration of a philanthropic association. The conversation revolved around several subjects which concerned the general welfare in industrial, scientific, and political respects. When it was thought that everything had been exhausted, one of the members stated that the noble intentions of the association could never be obtained as long as the religious principle did not rest on firmer foundations, and in this the proper rights were granted to reason.

You can easily think that such a remark drew the attention of the company to itself and will have brought about a wide-ranging debate. — Those present were honest Christians, and nevertheless a difference of views reigned as if you were speaking about the religion of the native inhabitants of Mexico. — One person denied reason any judgement over religious investigations. — Another claimed that it alone accounted for religion. — A third expressed that religion was absolutely not the matter of reason, but it must be able to be tested by this. — A fourth explained that religion was superfluous with a good state constitution in that it was at all times nothing more than a police institution intended for the weakness of human nature in order to provide more certain obedience to the arrangements of the state. — A fifth contradicted this all too cosmopolitan view and said that religion is necessary, but the existing Christian religion had outlived itself and did not fulfil its goal anymore. — This remark found absolutely no support, but was fought with such weak reasons that one person felt emboldened to declare that in order to produce a beneficent religion, Christ would have to be left entirely out of it; the time had come for it, the path of the clergy itself broken, and you must just not stand quiet now, time will toss out the old sourdough by itself and make space for purified views. — At this utterance too, as much as had the nature of the Christian religion been attacked, the contradiction which everyone shall have expected did not follow, and hence the utterances became by and by so free that a member of the company expressed the claim:

> "The image of Christ is not suited anymore to the gallery of the modern age, because the contours of its drawing contain such errors that they would not escape the eyes of the laypersons for much longer."

At this utterance a silence occurred. — Nobody had the courage to contradict, nor though to give applause. — Doctor Wehrmann used this silence and asked the company to give him their attention for a few moments.

The Parable

"The venerable company," he began, "knows my love for products of the plastic arts. This drove me to visit every place where the named art was especially flourishing. The Prince of D...t had a magnificent collection of such artworks from older and more recent periods. A significant number of artists stayed at his court constantly and satisfied the hobby of their princely patron with every effort of their in-born and trained talent. The prince bought everything which could to some extent pass as a work of art, and his museum, which consisted of an unusually large hall, filled up so much that there was barely place to be found for new products of art. The front part of the hall was taken up by the distinguished image of the Apollo Belvedere and served the whole as it were as a point of unity. The artists indeed had been urging for a long time already to be permitted to fill the large space of the front wall with pictures as well, only the prince wanted up to then to ignore them. Certainly the image, free from all cramped surroundings and at an appropriate elevation, looked so glorious that anyone who entered the hall was spontaneously carried away by admiration for this sun god and was drawn away from the other figures. It was thus not only the intention of the artists to obtain more space, but rather even if not to remove, at least to place in a less advantageous light such a dangerous rival.

The prince, tired of the frequent urging, assembled the artists about himself in the hall and said, Apollo remains the ornament of my art museum. There was nothing to be said against it, as it corresponded perfectly with the intentions of its master to portray him thus as he made the seven-toned lyre sound through the sunlit creation. — The prince fell silent. — One of the artists asked permission to express his views over the regularity of the named image. — The prince allowed it, and the artist began by making a few remarks over the correctness of the contours and drawing them into doubt. — Here, he said, the part of the arm is too short, back and loins have anatomical errors and indeed such that the thinking artist must often wonder how the image could have obtained such fame. — After several more had spoken in this sense, the prince replied, I have considered these small deviations up to now to be the intention of the artist who, in order to achieve the intended effect, had to shorten a little here and lengthen a little there. — But in order to show you that I am not persevering stubbornly in my views, I invite you to deliver me a better Apollo, and I promise you not only to restrict the space of this here, but to remove it from the hall. — One of the artists, and, by his pronouncement, not the worst, replied to this:

> "Lord! If this Apollo remains standing in this hall for as long as until a better one comes, then it will remain forever!" —

Here the narrator fell silent. — The company seemed shocked, for not a sound of applause or displeasure was to be heard. — Finally a voice asked, what applicability was to be drawn from this story? — The Doctor replied, "Finding the applicability I leave to the discernment of my well-disposed audience." — Since everybody fell silent again, High Court Justice Rink, an acknowledged sterling man, started to speak and said:

> "If the image of Christ in the gallery of founders of religion and all distinguished spirits of world history remains standing for as long as until a better one comes, then it will remain there eternally."

From this moment on the conversation of the company took on a formality and a seriousness so that one felt weird and left earlier than usual. — Even the valediction of the giver of the banquet was not hearty and thankful, but rather forced and cold, as if one would have been happy to finally be relieved of the obligation.

***

The Visit

A few days after this meeting, the Doctor received a visit from the Tax Assessor Selbach, who had also attended the above-mentioned evening banquet. He apologised on account of his intrusiveness, but explained that the story of the Apollo had made him think a lot, and, since he was incapable of sorting things out in his own mind, he had made the decision to seek out the narrator himself and to ask him to discuss the matter a little more specifically.

The Doctor rejoiced over the visit by a man of whom he had heard nothing but good. He offered him a chair, and after both had taken their places, he began.

"At the evening banquet a spirit showed itself which strayed entirely from the subject for whose sake people had come together. Unfortunately it is a common phenomenon of the so-called cultured society that, as soon as religion is spoken of, they become impassioned and scare off the spirit of an amusing or instructive conversation.

The Assessor replied here, "I have up to now held religion to be merely a matter of faith and, since opinion and faith are siblings, even synonyms, by necessity all outbreaks of differences of opinion must manifest, and cannot be anything but impassioned." — The Doctor responded, "When you claim opinion and faith have the same meaning, are synonyms, you say something which many have in common with you, but must be an obstacle, instead of being conducive to them on the path of research. — It is certainly true that what we think, we can also occasionally believe, just like how we often only think that which we feign to believe. — At first glance this idea surprises, but looked at more closely, the synonymity is repealed of itself. When I say I believe the first duty of humanity is to strive for truth, I am expressing a positive law of faith, an apparent conviction; for to want to say I think the first duty of humanity is to strive for truth strikes so much against our feeling that we recognise the word 'think' here to be saying absolutely nothing. Even the word 'know' can find no applicability here because knowing refers to the heard, taught, and learnt, or to sensory perceptions and ideas over which we can give a clear account, but which are incapable of imparting any information over the inner laws of life. — It cannot be said that I know the first duty of humanity is to strive for truth; because you cannot specify from where you know it. — If someone wanted to claim that he knew from his parents, his parson, or his teachers, then you would have to ask him, are you certain that your parents, the parson, or the teachers have not been deceived? — What could he answer? Nothing, but — I believe in the truthfulness of my parents, the parson, and my teachers. — Everywhere that it concerns inner, moral convictions, we have to rely on faith. Nobody can say who their parents are, because nobody is in a position to give an account over their procreation and birth. — But we are compelled to the truthfulness of it through the love of the parents, through an inner trait of disposition, and such a certainty is then called 'faith'. — There can be no talk here at all of opinion, because this would have to be called a demeaning of sacred feelings. Thus with much about opinion, faith, and knowing. — So long as the researcher is not agreed over these three designations, he will mix up the powers of life with one another and not be in a position to recognise any one spiritual power. — Hence, when various religious confessions are driven to hate and persecution, you should not imagine it happens because of a legitimate, better faith; no, it is the opinion, it is a haughty, apparent knowing of such who feel attacked and see without vigorous resistance their downfall before themselves."

Here the Doctor fell silent. — The Assessor, who had listened with great attentiveness, replied, "What you said is perfectly true and founded on the facilities of human nature in such a way that not the slightest reproach can be made to it. But it is also so subtle and delicate that it is not surprising why one so easily confuses opinion, faith, and knowing with each other. I see that in the clear difference of these three designations a security must lie for the researcher who is certain of their success. — But allow me to pass from this general analysis to my special matter and to ask you about the true interpretation of the parable which you placed before us via the story of the Apollo."

Doctor: "I wanted by the parable to bring the heterogenous views of the company under one idea."

Assessor: "Your tale referred to Christ?"

Doctor: "Yes."

Assessor: "Apollo is an image of the imagination and not of history."

Doctor: "Quite correct."

Assessor: "If Christ is only an image of the imagination, then what?"

Doctor: " If Apollo is also only a product of the imagination or of rapture, then it has a complete reality though. The artist carried it in himself, saw in himself its grandeur, perceived in himself the notes of the raised lyre, heard the harmony of the spheres, and gave in his image to the eye what was depicted living in his inner being."

Assessor: "All this leaves us still in the dark over the nature of Christ."

Doctor: "This examination alone enlightens us perfectly over the nature of Christ. — Where shall we have Christ? In us. — Where can we get to know him in spirit? In us. — History and dogma cannot satisfy us. — Indeed, if we saw him with our eyes, so long as he had not arisen in us we would not be able to comprehend him, we would not be able to believe him. — It is inconceivable how such truths are heeded so little, since one proceeds in everyday life in all branches of knowledge and capability according to these principles and considers nothing to be perfectly understood until it has passed into our own flesh and blood and come alive in us, indeed so that it occurs to us in the end as if we had been born with our arts and sciences."

Assessor: "That is surely true. But Christ is neither an object of the arts, nor of the sciences. We possess about him a rhapsodic story; and if we do not believe this, then he has not existed for us at all."

Doctor: "Christ, even if not known everywhere, belongs to humanity. His story begins with a first man, with an original son, fathered by God, and shines, by means of his spirit, through the Israelites' history until he personally appears. —

Adam, Seth, Enoch, Noah, Moses, David, and the prophets carried his spirit in themselves; were, before he himself had yet appeared, his confessors, and prepared his activity. — Christ himself said, before Abraham was, I was*; and gave by that sentence testimony that it was not about the person, but rather about a spirit residing in the man, about a divine light which a sublime person can surely fan, but not create."

Assessor: "Do you believe in the person of Christ?"

Doctor: "I must believe in it, if I shall not give the lie to reason and feeling."

Assessor: "What proof do you have?"

Doctor: "I could say, I carry the believability of his appearance in the heart; but this would be no proof for a coldly rational man. Hence I say, all epoch-making events of world history emanate from a sublime person. — Only Cyrus could make Asia subject to himself. — Only the genius of Alexander was able to conquer a part of Asia from Greece, to destroy the great power of Persia, and to stride across the Indus. — Only the strategic talent of a Julius Caesar was capable of placing Rome at the highest point of its power. Every great empire had its founder, every religion its originator. — Corporations are not suited to the accomplishment of great events, to the spread of prejudice destroying doctrine, because it is impossible that with many members the courage and unity reigns which is indispensable for any great undertaking. One must place themselves at the top, one must carry the burden of the undertaking and take on themselves the consequences, then great and extraordinary things can happen, whereas we see in the guild service of the corporations only ever the ordinary, never that which transcends mediocrity. — And the Christian religion which spread over all of Europe, over the greatest part of America, and over great stretches of Asia and Africa shall have been called into life by a company and a few writers? — Anyone who can claim that does not know history, does not know humanity, and has not yet even risen to an open opinion, still less to a firm belief."

Here the Doctor fell silent. — The Assessor said, "According to this discussion, here faith comes into play and must not

---

*   [Tr.: John 8:58.]

only replace knowledge, but strengthen it. — We cannot say after precise examination of the words that we know that Confucius, Zoroaster, Socrates, Plato, Alexander, and Julius Caesar lived; but we may believe in their having existed with unimpeachable conviction. — To want to deny the person of Christ means after this to stand against a necessity of nature without which Christianity could never have arisen. — I thank you for the light which you have given me and will certainly not make myself unworthy of it."

They spoke a bit to illuminate more closely what had been said and then parted, the Assessor with the request of being permitted to repeat his visit, the Doctor with the view of drawing a pearl from the dreary ocean of the world.

***

The Second Visit

For three weeks the Assessor digested what had been heard and came to the conclusion that, the simpler one judged a subject, the easier one found out the truth. — The person of Christ, which he had believed even a few weeks before to be contrary to reason, was now so clear to him that he claimed the consequences which arose from it could otherwise never have occurred without the greatest, supernatural miracle. — After he was no longer wavering in doubt over it, he decided to visit the Doctor again and ask for new explanations.

He went to the Doctor, but did not find him alone and wanted to immediately leave again. The Doctor bade him stay and introduced him to the presence of the Deacon Wohlfart with the remark that the latter was afflicted with the same malady as he was. — Turning to the Assessor, he said, "You come probably to provide me with a report of the results of your meditations, or to seek help over new doubts."

The Assessor replied, "You are right. I am here to tell you that I have thought about what was recently said and find myself completely reassured. Only I still have some other doubts which I do not know how to conquer, so that I must ask you to come to my aid with your accustomed kindness."

The Doctor asked them both to take a seat and, after he and his visitors had taken their seats, he began.

Doctor: "Now, what are the doubts which you are unable to master?"

Assessor: "The person of Christ is for me, according to the natural laws of faith, proven; only his effectiveness as lord and judge of the world seems to be drawn from such uncertain sources that, so long as I don't have information about it, I cannot yet number myself amongst the Christians."

Doctor: "You have touched on a point which many have already shrunk back from because one counts an influence of Christ on our life circumstances amongst those supernatural miracles which, without getting in the way of the course of nature, are absolute impossibilities. And yet such a one is not only possible, but even necessary, since without it the Christian religion would have no base and no test."

Assessor: "What, you really believe that Christ can now still hear and grant our requests?"

Doctor: "Indeed I believe it, and indeed not on the basis of orthodoxy, but rather from the necessity which lies in human nature."

Assessor: "If this knot can be naturally untied, then I must highly rebuke all philosophers who have taught and written about spirit and soul, over thinking and wanting, over transcendental and other concepts, and left us in ignorance over it."

Doctor: "Had to leave us in ignorance because they were not in a position to set Christianity in harmony with their systems and to raise it to a philosophical point of view."

Assessor: "Show me this philosophical point of view, and I will endeavour to force myself to it."

Doctor: "It will put you off if, in order to be thorough, I make use of Biblical texts. In the gospel of Matthew 12:31–32, Christ says, 'Wherefore I say unto you, All manner of sin and blasphemy shall be forgiven unto men: but the blasphemy *against* the *Holy* Ghost shall not be forgiven unto men. And whosoever speaketh a word against the Son of man, it shall be forgiven him: but whosoever speaketh against the Holy Ghost, it shall not be forgiven him, neither in this world, neither in the *world* to come.'

In the gospel of Mark 3:28–29, he says, 'Verily I say unto you, All sins shall be forgiven unto the sons of men, and blasphemies wherewith soever they shall blaspheme: But he that shall blaspheme against the Holy Ghost hath never forgiveness, but is in danger of eternal damnation'.

In the gospel of Luke 12:10, it states, 'And whosoever shall speak a word against the Son of man, it shall be forgiven him: but unto him that blasphemeth against the Holy Ghost it shall not be forgiven.'

Here it is talking about a spirit which we, at the loss of our self and an eternal salvation, must not sin against. — What sort of spirit is that? — Did it have a special habitation in the creation to which we should turn and seek it there; or is is it perhaps so close to us that we do not see it and recognise in it what the gospels comprehended under it because of its closeness? — Every thing in nature has its own, particular spirit which flows to it from all of creation as conforming power. — In every stone, every plant, every tree, every spring, every stream, every sea, every valley, every mountain, and in every animal a conformant spirit gathers which gives each of the named sorts form, colour, and being. — Is perhaps one of these spirits to be understood by the Biblical spirit? — That cannot be, in that none of them are subject to a sin and hence none also need any forgiveness. — Or are perhaps those spirits intended which humans draw from stones, herbs, fruits, wines, etc.? — That is just as impossible, since all these do without a positive life and consciousness and are also without sin. — Where now is the spirit which we must not blaspheme without causing our own downfall? — Is it in the heights, in the depths, in the air or in water? — It is everywhere, but concentrated in humanity it rises to an independence by means of which we think, feel, decide, and want, and hence can sin or omit it. — Is this surely the spirit which the Bible calls the holy one? — It must be, because it contains the highest within it, by which humanity can arrive at the freedom of an absolute independence. — But what now surely is the sin or the blasphemy against this holy spirit? — Oh, that one sways in doubt over it! — That humans can be so blind as to seek it outside themselves, in the heights, in history, in the reading of the Bible, or in the ceremonial service of some confession! — It is in us like the spirit of sweetness in the ripe grape. — It is in us like the spirit of the wine in its encasing fluidity. — It is in us like the gold in the interior of the mountain. — The light is golden matter; but one has never seen anywhere yet that pure gold flies around in the air or forms itself on the surface of the earth. — Deep under the earth the rays of light are concentrated as warmth, and since they seek an analogy, an image of the sun, their origin, to reflect themselves in and to attach to, they thus draw all similar things to themselves and form under the earth an image of the sun — gold. — I mean, such analogies should make comprehensible to humans what it is to have the holy spirit in yourself and to sin against it. — Nature is in front of us. It takes the same path everywhere, from seraph all the way to the little grain of sand in the desert. — Orthodoxy bristles indeed before such a natural doctrine. — To rationalism it remains a puzzle because rationalism's limitations leads it only to the threshold, but the spirit always remains closed to it. — We must be free; must stand midway between bigotry and rationalism and infer from the form the spirit, but from the spirit the necessity of form. — According to these views based on nature all objectivity is nullified; humans carry everything within themselves, against which they can sin, and hence it only concerns them themselves. — If all sins are forgiven, but only the sins against the spirit not, then humans need nothing but to know the will and the need of it in order to raise themselves to holiness and become creatures of the purest light."

Assessor: "You reveal to humanity by what you have said an outlook in which one looks out dizzily, but is incapable of grasping the extent of it."

Doctor: "How can we feel dizzy before a sight which draws our gaze within instead of outside us. The newness of the thing makes it seemingly difficult for us, but the performance requires only a firm will and persistence in order to obtain in time that which is not to be striven for in a moment."

Assessor: "But what is the sin against the spirit?"

Doctor: "When we limit it in its freedom, do not listen to its voice or its warnings, or even knowingly act against it."

Assessor: "How does the spirit admonish?"

Doctor: "Through reason and inner feeling. Through the former in that we by means of it can compare and examine what is good and evil, expedient or inexpedient, true or false. — But feeling carries in respect to pure human characteristics an incorruptible judge within itself, in that without doctrine from outside, it speaks to us an unmistakeable judgement over decency and indecency, over morality and bestial sensuality, over beauty and civility, over charm and vulgarity, indeed even over virtues and vices. — Between these two admonishers and guides, however, sensuality stands with its entire army of creaturely and worldly desires and seeks to captivate the natural judges, reason and feeling. — When reason is enticed to serve the creature and the temptations of the world, pride, envy, arrogance, avarice, obloquy, hate, falsehood, lies, irreligiosity and it appendices, and to distort

The Second Visit

with its calculus right into wrong, good into evil, then it sins against the spirit and itself summons it as judge against itself. — But feeling, and in it the conscience, which is only made silent with difficulty, sins as soon as it is numbed by the lure of sensuality, placated by misguided reason, and is itself drawn outwards by enjoying the delights of the senses. — Reason and feeling are the guides to the residence of the spirit. When these distract us from the proper path, we turn in sin against the spirit, which cannot be forgiven, neither here, nor there. — Not here because such a sin already on this side makes us weak, childish in age and dispirited so that we no longer have any means for reconciling the spirit or of making the spirit effective in us again, and, like a mummy, we wander about in a living death. — But from where shall the forgiveness come on the other side, if we squander our powers and time here, do not pay attention to our judge, the spirit, and have distanced ourselves so far from it that we can no longer feel or hear its admonishment and its words."

Here the Doctor fell silent. — Both his listeners seemed to have understood his views clearly, for each wanted at first to make remarks on it. — The Doctor, who became aware of this, said, "If you want to remark on what you have just heard, the Deacon is owed precedence because the subject falls primarily in his field." — The Deacon said the following: "Accustomed up to now to imagining the Holy Spirit in the image of a dove and hearing its voice coming down from heaven which, according to our ideas, is far above the clouds, I feel like someone fallen out of the clouds who seeks still in vain to set themselves on their feet without help. And yet I feel that it must be a comfortable state to stand on ones own feet. You have shown me the means of learning this art, and I promise to be a zealous student."

The Assessor, who likewise felt the urge to speak, expressed himself in this way: "What you have just said sounds so natural that one is almost tempted to believe one knew it already beforehand. — The office of judge, which the Christians conferred on the founder of the religion, is exercised by the spirit. It may be that we could call this spirit the Christ arisen in us, and then it is lord of our fate in that it judges over life and death. — Only according to the sense of the

Bible, it is not only a radiant, but also a rewarding, helpful, and instructive nature which orders our life circumstances, takes from our enemies the power to harm, and places storms and bad weather in the way in order to protect us and our property. — You have established the sin against the spirit as precedent condition in order to describe the dominion of Christ in its entire extent. Forgive me my immodesty. But the matter is too important, indeed I believe that with the production of such a rewarding world rule of Christ, Christianity would have to again grasp proper roots whereas it now has neither strength nor firmness."

The Doctor, who had expected this reply, now continued, "The premises are given; an expert thinker should know how to make the conclusions themself. And truly, the matter is so natural and simple that everyone would have to comprehend it if we had not been diverted so far from it by violence and by contrived cleverness. — With any spirit which is alive in us, with the spirit of that activity which we practise, in so far as this activity would be called into life by a person, you make use quite appropriately of the expression: the spirit of this or that inventor or founder is in us. Certainly here and there the spirits are different — the one is good, the other evil — one temporary, another eternal — one busies itself with worldly things, another with the divine. — Anyone now who decides to serve the divine and does this according to the principles of Christianity awakens the spirit of Christ, that is, awakens Christ in his spiritual potency in himself and has become a Christ. — We have just seen that the spirit, or as we now call it, Christ, appears against us as judge. If it can judge us, then it is also powerful enough to reward us. Indeed not coming into judgement is already a great benefit, but this does not yet satisfy our expectation in respect to protection and the reward for our fidelity. — To the spirit, to it, Christ in us, is given the power to provide for us in all the circumstances of life."

The Assessor fell into complete astonishment here over it and said, "What, so the human would by means of his spirit in himself be in a position to keep every misfortune at bay, to banish all evil from the people, and to produce the state of a general peace, a general bliss, in a word a state of paradise?"

The Second Visit

Doctor: "That the individual does not become capable of. He can smooth his own course and with enhanced facilities and practice extend his effectiveness on his environment. — But it is certain, if the greater part of the inhabitants of a land have awoken the spirit, that is, Christ, in themselves and not sinned against it, then over such a land no deformity, no destructive storms, no inundations, and no epidemic diseases would come."

The two listeners looked at him here with visible surprise. — The Deacon asserted that such an effect with such results would not be possible without the direct approval and intervention of God. — The Assessor countered, "I have an idea of to where our revered host, the good Doctor, is headed, but I already feel by the foreshadowing in such a state of surprise that I am looking towards the unravelling of this knot with true impatience."

The Doctor started speaking again and sought to satisfy the expectations of his two listeners in that he continued in the following way: "The spirit by means of which we can turn to God and eternity, can believe in God and eternity, and can make ourselves privy to the knowledge of God and of immortality is the purest, the highest that God placed in humanity. — What humans thus want to desire from God must happen through this spirit. This sublime spirit of God in us does not ask anymore, instead we must turn with our requests to it, then it will be aroused to activity, put itself in contact with all the powers all around which are related to it, bring them into its interests, act and create with them, draw them through the coarser elements down to our life path which it can smooth with them and lead us through seemingly impenetrable labyrinths. — These are the spiritual principles according to which the matter is explained. — Now we want to see, however, whether visible nature does not delivers us analogies by means of which we will have this spiritual activity before our eyes as it were.

A small cloud laden with electricity touches a larger one filled with moisture, and a lightning bolt occurs which startles humans and animals, tears trees from their roots, splits rocks, and shakes an entire area. — A small flame of light spreads brightness wide around itself. — The sound of a bell and a fire engine echoes through valleys, forests, and mountains. — The notes of music act far around themselves and attune the listener to the character of their melodies. — The power of attraction and repulsion of the poles is a miracle of nature which is not to be denied, but cannot be explained by any naturalist. — Since now the raw elemental powers bring forth such conspicuous effects, must we not conclude that a spiritual electricity, spiritual power of attraction, spiritual melodies, bound with the power of the spiritually living word, can achieve still greater things and call forth effects of a free will, a positive intention? — Doubting in such an activity means as much as if you wanted to say the moon, which receives its light, can surely illuminate, but the sun, which gives the light, is not capable of that. — I have said enough. Anyone who wants to grasp it, can; anyone, however, who does not have a firm will, for him all explanations are of no use and he will become, the more he hears, all the more timid."

The Doctor stood up, had a bottle of Malaga brought by his servant. After he had filled a glass for each, he said, "We stand at the foot of a high mountain and need strength to climb it. To a happy arrival at the top!" — They drank. — The Deacon placed his glass on the table and said with somewhat doubtful demeanour, "According to what was said, did Elijah carry in himself the sparks with which he ignited the fire of heaven which consumed the head people over fifty?"*

Doctor: "Quite certainly."

Deacon: "And did Elisha by means of his own spiritual power return to life the son of the Shunammite and perform his miracles?"†

Doctor: "No different."

Deacon: "And did Christ command the raging sea and the storms to be calm through his own inner spiritual power?"‡

Doctor: "Indubitably."

Deacon: "Doctor! You have set me, and probably also my friend here, in a new world in which we do not yet know where we should look, and what language one speaks."

---

* [Tr.: 2 Kings 1:9–15.]
† [Tr.: 2 Kings 2:18–37.]
‡ [Tr.: Matthew 8:26; Mark 4:39; and Luke 8:24.]

The Second Visit

Doctor: "In the world in which we are resolved to enter, you speak the language of the spirit, the language of the Christians whose ABC does not sound without, but rather within, and forms there through spiritual elements a language which is the word of God, of Christ himself, and can thereby lead, advise, and guide us victoriously through all obstacles."

The Assessor did not seem to be as disturbed as the Deacon by what had been said, because he knew nothing about all the theological theses and antitheses and hence was yet closer to nature. — Thus he spoke briefly: "Christ will rule the world as soon as all humanity recognises the spirit and does not sin against it. — Christ leads the relationships of our life if we find in ourselves the spirit, which is eternal, and entrust ourselves to it. — Thank you, Doctor, my dear patron and benefactor, for the light which you have given me, and I promise that I will entertain it like a vestal flame for whose extinguishing the penalty was set of being buried alive. I will not be buried alive, but am instead resolved to rise from the dead."

This declaration gave the Doctor joy. But he encouraged the Deacon with the following words: "You feel yourself transposed into a new land since I want to lead you to the elements of life and of wisdom! — That amazes me, in that you, a Pestalozzian*, should have long since been accustomed to seek the elements from every matter and to proceed from these to knowledge and practice. — But, your spiritual disposition bristles still from going to work in such sublime things in an elemental way, whilst I can assure you in all that is sacred to me that for humanity no positive salvation is to be obtained if it does not happen in this way. All branches of knowledge and capability rest on specific, irrevocable elements. — You can only count with numbers, measure with lines, make music with notes, paint with colours. — Someone who wants to learn wisdom without having awoken the language elements in themselves seems to me like a child who wanted to count without numbers, measure without circle, protractor, and ruler, make music without notes, and paint without colours. — You will think these analogies are exaggerated! — But you

---

* [Tr.: Johann Heinrich Pestalozzi (1746–1827) was a Swiss educational reformer who emphasised education of the whole child.]

say yourself, where do we seek wisdom? — Answer: in the clouds, in writings, and don't think at all as if here a beginning, a root were to be found from which fruits of a higher spiritual knowledge could come, knowledge which would provide us with enlightenment over God and immortality."

The Deacon responded, "Show me the root." — The Doctor replied, "As soon as you once see the necessity that only on this path is a goal to be obtained, then I will show you the elements in so far as they do not occur to you yourself; until then I admonish you to be patient and to trust in the spirit, or in Christ within you, who will be a merciful judge of all who seek him."

Both visitors left soon after this and admired the Doctor's abundance of spirit which was capable of speaking about such subtle subjects always with new images. — The Doctor released them with the assurance that the source of the spirit, once it flows, is inexhaustible.

***

The Alliance of Friendship

When the Assessor and the Deacon had left the Doctor, they took a walk into the outskirts of the town in order to mutually discuss what they had heard. The Assessor told his companion of the manner of his acquaintance with the Doctor, and described to him thereby the impression which his story about the image of Apollo had made on him and a part of the company at the banquet. The Deacon responded, "The Doctor seems, next to his superb character, to possess yet another innate talent of turning any event to use for the most elevated need of mankind, for religion. He gained me at a music lesson in Pestalozzi's manner. — I do not know whether you yourself are a musician, and know of this new way of teaching music or not." — After the Assessor had answered in the negative, the Deacon continued.

"You have heard that the Doctor pointed me in learning wisdom always to the elements. This refers to our first meeting at a lesson by the aforesaid method. — Here one teaches at the start nothing but the elements of music, that is, notes and relations of beat. — You let the student sing the scales with numbers by and by and do not concern yourself with the hitherto usual naming. The beat is subject to an apparent mechanism in which one has brought all the relations of time into specific forms and has them exercised for as long as until the student, penetrated by the beat, can no longer do anything but have everything sound in the most correct time. In this way the students learn the thing by playing and at the same time as fundamentally as is possible in no other way in such a short time. — The system which describes the relationships of notes and beat with names now becomes a necessity for them, and indeed so much so that, if you placed nothing in front of them, they would themselves make one. I often visited these lessons in order to make my own this method, and one day met the Doctor who was listening to the students with great attentiveness. He was testing the method with the thoroughness of a man who was not to be blinded by the shimmer of superficiality, and asked the teacher in various instances for some explanation. But as for this the latter did not possess the language skills to explain the matter briefly and thoroughly, I undertook this business and explained to the Doctor everything as much as the shortness of the time allowed. He listened to my explanations with pleasure, requested from the teacher a few more tests of this elemental process and took his leave after expressing his thanks to him and the students. He turned to me, however, with the question, 'What do you think, man of religion, what would surely come about if you also treated theology in this manner and taught the candidates in the elemental way instead of filling their heads with words, theses, and often unintelligible dogma, and stepped from the elements to the matter and to the spirit?'

I answered that if such a process were possible, it would have to admittedly be of great success. But since theology has dictated too much, and the practice would have to be derived from this, it would be necessary to first have names and a system in order to be able to seek the matter in this. To this he responded, 'If that is so, then the religion does not originate out of the eternal.' — I was a bit embarrassed and said, 'The religion was given to us by God.' — 'Quite right,' he said, 'as God and eternity are one here. And if this is the case, then it can only be revealed by a positive gift which all humans possess, and must, like here with the music, also be learned in an elemental way.' — I wanted to say something, but did not know straightaway what. — He saw my embarrassment and parted, saying to me trustingly, 'More about that another time.'"

The Assessor, who had already previously been filled with boundless respect for the Doctor, felt still more excited by the simple image of the music lessons. — "What sort of a man is that, the Doctor," he said, "who from all that he encounters knows how to draw light, whilst we, thinking ourselves quite clever, see nothing but the passing phenomena! — Music lies within humans so that they, without any instruction and without previously having known what music is, must sing. — Indeed, music is as it were present in nature so that even if the human were too stupid to hear and to feel its melodies, the birds of the forest would not fall silent and would join in the song of the spheres. — Music is eternal; numbers are eternal; the lines of geometry are not invented; logic lies in our ability to think; the feeling for law and order and decency are inborn characteristics of humanity. — Everywhere we find the eternal thing, and therefore the religion which is only occupied with eternity cannot be a creation of time, of history, of invention, or even of just a temporary need. — But where are the elements of this original thing to be found, this thing by means of which you arrive at your goal safely?"

The Deacon, for whom the elemental way lay close to his heart, agreed with this and said, "It it just this indeed which also disturbs me, because I do not see any light anywhere which could show me the way to the elements of a true wisdom. — I am a clergyman, and therefore the answering of such questions is more natural for me than for anyone else. — How can I fulfil my difficult calling if I know only the dead letters, but not the spirit of our religion? — If I imagine the Doctor to be a clergyman, how would he have to be able to teach and preach? He would know how to give references and images in inexhaustible abundance, whereas we, with our ponderous book learning, continue to chew on what we extracted days ago from books or from memory."

The Assessor, seeing the difficulty of the position of a clergyman, encouraged his companion to follow all the more firmly the views of the Doctor, as they were at the same time required by his life's calling. — The Deacon said, "I will follow so closely that nothing might separate me anymore. — But what sort of prospects will I then have? — Then I will stand alone and find no soul who can share my desolation. — How will my fellow clergy see me when I follow neither the pietists, nor the rationalists? — These two parties are now in control and — although of quite opposing views — both are so powerful that each is afraid of the other and therefore leaves them in peace. But if someone should dare to strike out on a new path between the two, they would set upon them and destroy them morally."

The words enlightened the Assessor, and he made an effort to brighten the darkness of this prospect and said, "Your fellow clergy can forsake you, but the matter remains for you. It is above opinions and human statutes, according to the little we know of it, and can give compensation if envy and stupidity offend you. — And if the assurance that you should find a friend in me who will not ever abandon the path I have recently set out on can give you courage, then count under all circumstances on my sympathy and, if it is necessary, on my assistance." — The Deacon responded, "I accept your offer, and as young as our friendship may yet be, it is reinforced by the seal of a striving for positive, eternal, religious truth resting on itself."

With these words the bond of friendship was concluded, resting not, as is common, on momentary elations, but rather on the feeling of a striving which, aiming at eternal laws, promised the bond an eternal duration. They returned to the city, and before they parted from one another, they gave each other their word to record all that had previously been said and their views over it, to discuss it, and thus in the exchange of ideas to test their progress, to exercise their new-found powers, and to then put them in action. — They kept their word. Each wrote something down about the day which could order and explain his views. — For the Deacon, the Pestalozzian music instruction was the lodestar of his inquiries, and even if he could not yet find the elements, the simplicity of the method preserved him from the deceptions which so easily tempt us in spheres where we do not see nature anymore and seek reality in vain in an ideal realm. — The Assessor by contrast endeavoured to idealise the person of Christ in order to explore the general law in an ideal placed at the highest peak and to educate himself accordingly. — Anyone will realise by themselves that this second path, which is set out on by so many, leads rarely however to a goal, and must be far more difficult than the first because you easily lose yourself in the clouds when climbing up to the peak and no longer know the laws of time. Both men made progress, however, and had a beneficial effect on each other. — The Deacon drew the Assessor down from his idealised height, the latter though kept the former above the mist of all too pedantic elemental activity which hinders the living genius in the end with utterly technical and logical orderliness from obtaining its freedom and leading us to self-knowledge. —

The Alliance of Friendship

Through this interplay they became, without speaking about it, the most intimate friends and felt thereby already rewarded many times over for the striving after unadulterated truth.

***

Fragments

It would be rambling to offer here everything which the two friends wrote down; however individual fragments will be gladly read by anyone in order to see how their views expand, how their spirit develops, and how it leads them to the point of being able to say: here we stand on the boundary which you cannot cross without guide or without the cooperation of a power awakening in us. Let us hear first the words of the Assessor where he seeks to provide light on the nature of the Christian religion.

"The Christian religion exists. — I am a Christian. — But what am I in that I am a Christian? — The most essential thing seems to consist of being a participant in a higher civilisation than we see with other confessions of faith. Certainly I obtained a great joy from it and it would be sinful not to be thankful, especially if you consider in what brutishness most non-Christian peoples still languish. — But, I ask, does this merit belong to Christianity alone, or are not the accidental institutions of state also responsible for it? — Greece stood at the highest degree of culture and did not consist of Christians. Its works of art and in part its philosophy surpass ours by far. If I had lived at the time, what would have been different about me or in me? — Or if my parents in the same state in which I now live had belonged to the Jewish religion, and I had become a Jew, I would surely have thought differently, felt and wanted differently? — There is no question that each confession delivers a different outward stamp, but that is only accidental and the consequence of social circumstances. — My feeling, thinking, hoping, and loving would certainly be no different than they are now, and from that I must conclude that Christianity, or the spirit of it by means of which Christ could say, before Abraham was, I was[*], contains something quite different than the usual forced interpretations, perhaps a force of nature, a natural disposition of humans which we

---

[*]   [Tr.: John 8:58.]

seemed to have lost and which do not even know the name of anymore."

Another time it went:

"To the extent Christianity does not lie as a disposition in humans, it has no general interest and cannot spread across the surface of the earth. — But as soon as a natural disposition must be considered, then we lack nothing but the key principle in order to know what this disposition consists of so that we can in fact inform humanity about it again. Believing, hoping, and loving are splendid, I would like to say divine, feelings, but they are not denoted by the name 'disposition', because thereunder is understood constantly a natural ability or skill which refers to artificial and scientific attributes. — Faith, hope, and love are feelings which warm the life, but give it no higher scientific standpoint. Should these feelings amount regardless of this to the desired disposition? — Should that Christ be contained in this who was Abraham before? — The matter becomes more and more involved, the more I inquire into it."

***

The Deacon, from whom here a few things shall be offered, went to work more easily without though becoming master of all his doubts. For him the Pestalozzian teaching method, which splits the matter into its elements and then expertly reassembles them, remained the norm for his inquiries, and he said in this respect:

"Religion is innate to humanity, must be innate to it, otherwise they would not have it. — For that we do not possess any powers, any elements, we do not attain it, and even if we were to make the most indescribable effort. — We cannot fly, for the simple reason that we have no wings; had we wings, however, then nature would teach us to fly. — Where now are the natural powers of humanity which draw it to religion? — What are the elements which, reassembled, amount to religion? Anyone who could contrive here a Pestalozzian method, how many mistakes would he free us from! — But we wander about thus in a great whole without knowing what it consists of. We are like the layman who hears a great piece of orchestral music, but does not comprehend what power holds together the various instruments. — I see the enormous space and countless worlds within it. — What is the scale of these worlds? — The worlds and their creatures move according to a proper tempo — by what beat do they move? — If we leave this infinity, however, and merely investigate the powers of humans which collect from nature the elements, and — as with the music which also fills the entire space — can adapt to our personality, what shall we seek in the area of religion, and what elements can we find which underlie the phenomena of the Bible and which bring them to light as productions of art? — I am entering a labyrinth where I see no exit and almost despair at the possibility of ever finding one."

After the doubt had ensnared him again after such inquiries, and he was at a loss to help himself, he got his displeasure off his chest in the following way:

"There is nothing more humiliating for a human than to live always in doubt. Many of my colleagues get this unbearable condition off their chest by denying instead of doubting. — But what do they obtain by that? — Nothing; less than nothing; for to see before yourself a certain downfall, a certain entrance into an eternal night is the most horrible thing a human can think of. The human must be able to dispose of his doubt, but not by denial and disbelief, only then may he consider himself a creature who has perfect cause to rejoice over being born with understanding and reason."

He expressed himself in such a way in his written investigations and returned again and again to that the basic lesson of religious laws must be traced back to basic elements, as music is traced back to scale and beat, to the extent religion is given as a free gift of the Creator for the free use of humanity.

***

A New Acquaintance

The Doctor, who had meanwhile been making excursions, partly by carriage, partly by foot, into the countryside, had used a beautiful afternoon to go for a walk and found himself quite alone in the garden of a tavern which was about one and a half hours from the city. He had bought a bottle of wine and a simple sandwich and now let his spirit reign undisturbed in the open countryside. Hardly had he spent half an hour in this calm preoccupation, than a well-dressed and well-educated man came into the garden, ordered wine and bread, and sat down at another table, but close by. The man, when he had received his wine, observed the Doctor with special attentiveness, as if he wanted to recall whether and when he had already seen him. The Doctor, whom this did not escape, and who was seeking for that reason to start a conversation, stood up as if he wanted to take a walk through the garden, but said, as he came alongside his garden neighbour:

Doctor: "The beautiful weather has enticed you too into the countryside?"

Stranger: "Anyone who has professional business must make use of the free hours."

Doctor: "Why do you not go to a place then which is visited more than this one?"

Stranger: "I have been coming here already for many years and also consider the changing of taverns to be a sort of disloyalty which you should not end up guilty of without reason."

Doctor: "Loyalty is a beautiful virtue, and anyone who already exercises it in the small things, in the choice of taverns, shows that you can rely on them."

Stranger: "I did not speak of loyalty in order to receive a compliment, but rather to give a honest answer."

Doctor: "Anyone who speaks well without reflecting bears the goodness in themselves and can support themselves on their words."

Stranger: "Dear sir, your remarks are of a sort that I am convinced you are the one I consider you to be."

Doctor: "Whom do you consider me to be?"
Stranger: "Doctor Wehrmann."
Doctor: "That I am. From where do you know my name?"
Stranger: "My friend, the Assessor Selbach, has spoken with me about you a few times already."
Doctor: "Selbach does me the pleasure of occasionally visiting me."
Stranger: "And you repay that pleasure with good instruction."
Doctor: "He trusts in me."
Stranger: "That is true; for he claims you have given him the key to a life view which he could not have received without you."
Doctor: "We press ahead with the teachings of nature in a peculiar way."
Stranger: "By means of which you are not only becoming familiar with nature, but also with its creator."
Doctor: "We do not separate nature from the creator and nor the creator from the created."
Stranger: "Those are peculiar, I would like to say new, views."
Doctor: "There are temporal, but also eternal peculiarities. The temporal refer to a nation, to a corporation, or to an individual human. The eternal belong to humanity."
Stranger: "What might declare which belongs to humanity and which only to a part or an individual?"
Doctor: "Reason, understanding, the feeling and the consciousness that we are."
Stranger: "This view penetrates me too deeply. I am not so teachable as the Assessor."
Doctor: "Then you need a bit longer to get to the truth than he does."
Stranger: "Positive truth must be quickly comprehended."
Doctor: "Eh, so tell me though, why can one comprehend a thing, but others also not comprehend it?"
Stranger: "Those whom it enlightens comprehend it, those whom it does not enlighten do not comprehend it."
Doctor: "Accordingly a thing can be true without it being comprehended by everyone."

A New Acquaintance

Stranger: "You are right. My remark does not have complete applicability."

Doctor: "You seem not only to be loyal, but also to be indulgent, because you do not persist with your remark."

Stranger: "I seek truth, and there obstinacy is no good, regardless of my nature possessing a stubbornness which wants to see with its own eyes."

Doctor: "That is good as long as you have achieved a certain maturity. In the beginning it is obstructive."

Stranger: "That I believe. But I cannot change my nature."

Doctor: "That would also not be good, because the nature must instruct us."

Stranger: "How does the nature instruct?"

Doctor: "Through forms, colours, and movement."

Stranger: "But how do we learn to understand colours, forms, and movement?"

Doctor: "Here I cannot answer further because, if I said the truth, you would be surprised and probably lose trust."

Stranger: "Is it right to keep the truth secret?"

Doctor: "No. But you should share it cautiously in order not to deter."

Here the stranger drank a drop of wine; but the Doctor looked at his watch as if he wanted to check the time which remained to him for further debate. — They spoke now again about the weather, about the service at the tavern, and the practicality of the road leading past. — The Doctor himself went back to his table to drink a drop of wine and eat a bite of bread. The stranger went with him, and both sat down at the Doctor's table as if they had an important business to settle. — It lasted a long time until the discourse again became interesting. — The Doctor asked with whom he actually had the honour of speaking. The stranger introduced himself as Professor Solbring, who had already been eager for a long time to make the acquaintance of Doctor Wehrmann. The Doctor returned this courtesy and the following discourse began:

Doctor: "You seem to have entertained expectations of me which are seldom realised in personal contact."

Solbring: "I must confess that my expectation is quite eager, in that you have spoken with the Assessor about subjects of the greatest importance and indeed in a way which surprises on account of its newness."

Doctor: "I investigated the attitudes of the Assessor in order to learn whether he was a Christian, or must yet become one."

Solbring: "And the result?"

Doctor: "Was doubtful."

Solbring: "He was baptised, confirmed, and raised Christian, thus he must be a Christian."

Doctor: "I know a man who knows all the stars in the sky with their names and yet is no astronomer."

Solbring: "There are certainly phenomena where you think to possess with the name the thing as well."

Doctor: "Yes, and unfortunately I must extend this still further and say that these phenomena are so frequent that they amount to the majority amongst humanity."

Solbring: "This claim I would not like to agree with unconditionally."

Doctor: "Wordy erudition has for the most part conquered the realm of knowledge, the memory is lord, and a proper, innate knowledge, which alone wisdom and philosophy is, is hardly spoken of anymore."

Solbring: "You can teach the memory-knowledge, the innate you must leave to each themselves."

Doctor: "And nevertheless you teach music which is innate to humanity. You teach counting, calculating, measuring, and comparing — abilities which all lie in our nature and become active by themselves."

Solbring: "You are right. But how are these natural dispositions applied to religion, since it is something that arose in time and is imperative in it?"

Doctor: "Religion, that is, the system, arose in time, but its nature, its spirit is of eternity."

Solbring: "The imperative religion is accordingly a form in which we should seek the spirit."

Doctor: "So it is."

Solbring: "But is the form of the sort that can have contained in it by necessity the spirit and no other?"

Doctor: "The question is good, but so important that I cannot foresee how it can be discussed in as short a time as we still have before us today."

Solbring: "Then I want to ask another question. The Assessor told me you claimed God hears the request of anyone who can turn to him in spirit. Does that not conflict with the unity of God? — If God is only one, then he has an independent, self-contained ego. This ego I can probably divide according to time, but not according to space."

Doctor: "How do you get that?"

Solbring: "God by means of the unity of his ego cannot be divided up so that he, in the moment when he hears a request in India, can give his attention also at the same time to a request in America, Spain, France, Germany, or other regions."

After this remark, the Doctor took the Professor by the arm, asked him to follow him for a few steps and, after he had moved him out of the shade and had set his countenance towards the sun, he said, "See the sun there in the sky. It appears to the eye like a small disc, notwithstanding which it warms and illuminates the entire globe. If you have on one day all the inhabitants of the earth place themselves in the sunlight to warm themselves, then each will feel the full influence as if he were alone. — Yes, give each yet a magnifying glass with which he collects the rays of the sun in order to set something alight which lies before him, then no single one will receive less, and no plant, no little flower, neither in the gardens, nor in the fields, is cut short. — Since now the sun, this little disc in the universe, is capable of such things, must we not then by necessity conclude that the eternal sun of life which fills the entire universe, that God in his immeasurability must be even less limited than the sun disc, and even more so than the latter capable of giving light, life, and hearing to everyone who places themselves in his light and turns the magnifying glass of a sincere heart to him? — When we separate him, the eternal, from us, then we distance him from his light, and our request becomes an empty play of the tongue to which no granting can be accorded."

Solbring: "Consequently would the entire universe be nothing more than an eternal sun of life?"

Doctor: "So it is."

Solbring: "And this sun would be God?"

Doctor: "Nothing other than."

Solbring: "And we and all the parts of creation, all the suns and worlds are in him?"

Doctor: "We in him, and he in us."

Solbring: "I am astonished and comprehend according to the literal sense, but the immensity of the thought hinders me from getting a clear idea."

Doctor: "That I well believe. Continually accustomed to personifying and individualising, we can only with difficulty raise ourselves to an overarching, general concept. With such business the comparison to ideas you have seen and heard does not suffice. Here feeling must take over the main activity and tell us what is beautiful and good, great and sublime."

Solbring: "According to that, in order to form concepts feeling is as necessary as seeing and hearing."

Doctor: "As you can only doubt. Someone who does not feel the magic of music does not know what music is. — For someone who does not feel the stimulus and the concordance of the colours, how can they know what painting is? — Someone who does not feel God can never comprehend his power, his wisdom and kindness, and will also never share in him."

The Professor did not know how to respond to this and seemed at once to sink into contemplation. The Doctor, who did not want to disturb him, rang for the waiter in order to ask for the bill. — The Professor, for whom it also seemed to be time to go home, said, "If it does not burden you, then I will accompany you." — The Doctor was agreeable to this proposal. They walked together, spoke along the way of various things about what had been said above, and parted, on the part of the Professor with the request to be permitted to visit him (the Doctor) from time to time. — The Doctor gave the assurance that he would be always welcome; and so they parted with the feeling of having lived through a few pleasant and at the same time instructive hours.

***

The Third Parable

The Doctor had gone on a journey on account of family matters, and for that reason the two friends remained for almost two months reliant on themselves in their inquiries. — He had only been back a few days, without them knowing, and they were pleasantly surprised when they found him on a building site where carpenters were busy putting up a house. He was observing with pleasure the present work where you build up a house from beams in the air without any other means of connection than crossbeams. The two friends hurried up to him, greeted him, and asked whether they might soon burden him with a visit. He responded, "that can happen straightaway, only we want to see the gable concluded beforehand." — The master carpenter had meanwhile come to them and expressed his joy over the interest which the gentlemen were taking in his work. — The Doctor was straightaway drawn into a conversation with him and said, "It is not easy for the observer to get a more interesting sight than to see a house being erected by expert carpenters; how they know to join and connect a dispersed material so expertly that you could believe they had a magic spell to put it all together so securely. Don't be offended if I ask on which laws this art rests?"

Master: "Sir, you are asking something which you certainly know as well as I do. Though if it is about hearing how we speak about the matter, then I must tell you that the entire art lies in the correct knowledge of the St Andrew's cross[*]. Such a thing carries, connects, pushes from itself so that you can build through its correct use as high as you want. The beams of the said cross do not even always need to hit or lie against each other in order to fulfil their aim, to the contrary, you separate the four beams arbitrarily, but so that each individual one remains with the three others in respect to its

---

[*] [Tr.: an X-shaped cross.]

bearing and binding in a precise relationship, and for any one that pushes to one side a counter effect is put on the others."

Doctor: "But on what law does the security of such a connection rest?"

Master: "On the law of gravity."

Doctor: "Then it must take a lot of effort to make that understandable to the workers."

Master: "There you make no effort, they must learn to comprehend it themselves when they prepare the beams for it."

Doctor: "Self-comprehension! — You would barely hold it to be possible. We scholars think you cannot comprehend any matter without first getting a long, school-like explanation."

Master: "Because of that the scholars only build houses of paper, in which nobody can live and warm themselves; but we do so from beams whose gaps are closed and fastened."

Doctor: "Now, and the stonemasons?"

Master: "The stonemasons don't actually need to comprehend anything at all except that the stones are heavy and fasten themselves through pressure."

Doctor: "Accordingly your handiwork demands more science than that of the stonemason?"

Master: "Admittedly, in so far as we must set and connect together, but they only need to set together."

Doctor: "And no explanation is given to the stonemasons either?"

Master: "As little as the carpenters. Someone who does not learn to understand it themselves is unusable; but those who comprehend it once do not think that it was anything but innate to them, and cannot understand anymore at all the state when he had not yet comprehended it. For that reason even those who cannot yet grasp it are given the coarsest nicknames of dumbness and stupidity."

Doctor: "Thank you for your friendly instruction and I will also seek to introduce such a process to my own work."

He left with his two friends and went with them to his apartment. Arriving there, they expressed their joy over the unplanned reunion. But he said, "Now we will have to seek to capture again what we missed."

The Third Parable

The two friends handed over to the Doctor their written essays. He read a bit in them and said, "Writing is good, for it requires us, if we are at an end with learned knowledge, to seek in ourselves and to express something in free, even thought. — — As soon as we have once come to be able to draw not only from the sources of others, but rather from our own sources, we are on the trail of the matter and must come to the realisation.

You, my dear friend Selbach, have been induced by the story of the artist who wanted to have removed the most beautiful image, the Apollo, from the museum to think in an expert way about the founder of the Christian religion. You have felt in the sublime image of Christ, even if only an ideal, the spirit of Christianity and learnt to recognise it, how much more would this have to be the case when you have convinced yourself that the image is not only an idea, but rather a portrait. — There is no question; only unusual dispositions of art and spirit are capable of projecting a sublime ideal; regardless of this, an original stands far above the ideal, because we see in that one the most sublime idea made real. But for us even the portrait again becomes an ideal because that is given to us for imitating, though it stands so high that we look at it in astonishment and must be content to resemble it only a little. This path is according to the sayings of older wise men certain, only the hardest because the purity of a mere idea must reform our inner being and as it were awaken to action by a spiritual sublimation the purest within us.

You, my dear clergyman, think that if you could dissolve religion, like music, into its elements and practise them, then if not all, at least much would be gained for the matter. I agree with you and even claim that so long as we are incapable of this the Christian church still rests on unstable piles. — The idealists are incapable of giving the church the appropriate firmness because their activity is far too ethereal to draw a theory from it. For that reason we do not want to tire until we succeed in finding such a sort of instruction which can satisfy those who have a thirst for divine truth.

We discovered with the master carpenter another sort of instruction which surpasses everything that methods alone can achieve. — Here there is no teaching at all. From the mechanics of physical activity, the concept, the spirit must evolve. In this way you practise a matter first and then the cause explains itself. This is also an elemental process, but still simpler than the Deacon wishes. — Here everything rests on the being able, because without such no positive knowledge in conceivable. According to this principle you must first know how to count before you calculate. You must yourself be able to swim in order to specify in what way the limbs must be active for it. Only those who can fence know what the art of fencing is. Only the trained artist has a clear idea of the spirit of his art. — Would we after these inferences, to which a good many could be added, be making a conclusion too rashly if we said only the Christian, that is, only the person privy in practice to the nature of Christianity, is capable of recognising and comprehending the spirit of it? — Seen from this side, we know also straightaway what we have to think about the writings which speak against Christianity. — They are written by illiterates who are like the weak person who calls anyone an enthusiastic fool who believes in the art of swimming, since indeed man has no flippers. — Here only the words are lacking in order to explain myself convincingly enough, and that is why the categorical principle may suffice: that nobody can comprehend any matter before he has practised it. — Certainly we upset the operation of the current teachers of religion completely, where they think to educate the spirit by explanations. — Catechisms learnt by rote, alongside other religious and Biblical sayings, spoken with a pious demeanour, comprises the Christian nowadays; they want nothing to do with the prescribed tests of Christianity, and the most Christian person who takes the field against defamers of the gospels with fire and sword is easier to bring to accuse the evangelists of a false view than to confess the truth of the prescribed tests of a pure Christian faith.

You will be surprised that you hear me speak of tests of which you have probably heard nothing about in your life, which you have perhaps read without noticing, and of which every teacher of religion takes good care not to speak, from fear it might even occur to his listeners to also call for them. — I will recite to you the prescribed tests and then ask you whether you have ever heard anything clearer, more concise,

The Third Parable

and logically more correct. They are the verses 15, 16, 17, and 18 in the 16ᵗʰ chapter of the Gospel of Mark and go like this:

> And he said unto them, Go ye into all the world, and preach the gospel to every creature.
> He that believeth and is baptized shall be saved; but he that believeth not shall be damned.
> And these signs shall follow them that believe; In my name shall they cast out devils; they shall speak with new tongues;
> They shall take up serpents; and if they drink any deadly thing, it shall not hurt them; they shall lay hands on the sick, and they shall recover.

The tests of true Christianity are not to be described more clearly. And it is not surprising that in a time where such are completely missing, the matter loses its worth and is seen and treated as a temporal institution of the state. — Driving out devils, talking in new tongues, banishing snakes, drinking deadly things without harm, and finally by the laying on of hands on the sick, even if not healing, alleviating, they are the things which everyone should be able to perform who lays claim to a post of chairman or teacher of theology and to the Christian church."

The Deacon was surprised and asked, "Do the verses say just that in the Bible?" — The Doctor said, "If a clergyman asks, then it is not to be held against the layman if he does not know it." — The Doctor opened the Bible lying on his desk and gave him the verses to read. — After the Deacon had done so with eyes flying across the page, he said, "Truly, there it is word for word.

> And these signs shall follow them that believe; In my name shall they cast out devils; they shall speak with new tongues; etc.

To the extent it is true that those who do not believe shall be damned, so too are all damned who cannot do such deeds. — It is natural that, since everything in the world has its tests, such a thing in the most important affair of a human's life, in its religious effects, must not be lacking. — Someone who also says he believes, and is incapable of confirming their belief by such works, has a false faith and is damned. — I confess that I speak my own sentence of damnation by this confession, but thanks to our teacher, the good Doctor, for the good deed of having shown me clearly the position in which I find myself, and I will endeavour to be able to some day step up to the test."

The Doctor replied, "I wanted to lead you to the edge where there is no more holding back, but rather where you are forced by necessity to step forwards or backwards. — A bold wanderer does not go backwards, and hence we want to offer each other our hands happy in mind and go steadfast towards the time of the test."

The Doctor did not let himself get drawn into any further explanations anymore, and they parted in the feeling of an inexorable necessity of steadfastly strolling along the entered path.

**

The Relative

The Assessor was a nephew of the Dean Blumhof, a respected and, on account of his canonical strictness, very esteemed clergyman. The latter had learnt that the former was associating with Doctor Wehrmann, whom he suspected of atheism and freemasonry. For this reason he came to the capital for once in order to convince himself over the matter and to break the said contact. He was received by the Assessor, who suspected nothing less than a sounding out in this visit, with hearty joy and with all that he had at his command and could give pleasure to his worthy guest, and was entertained and fed. — After the meal, when the coffee had already been drunk, and the wife of the Assessor had left the dining room for a period to sort out everything else which was needed, the Dean came out with the intention of his visit and asked the Assessor in what association he stood with Doctor Wehrmann. — The questioned man, not suspecting any harm, gave a frank report and first became aware at the conclusion of his report of the dark demeanour of his uncle. The latter was not concealing his annoyance any longer and elaborated his concerns in the following way.

"My dear boy! You know your mother was my sister. We have always entertained a cosy family relationship amongst all the members of my father's house. Your mother and I were especially well disposed to each other, for every event in her family I had to share with her, rejoicing with the happy and showing my sympathy with the sad. — I was already in office when you went to the high school for the first time, and I still recall that day as a family festivity which was celebrated by your parents. — At the time I promised to watch over and tend to both your temporal and your eternal fortunes. — I have kept my word, and you have rewarded my interest through diligence and good behaviour. — I saw you, since I have no children, as my son who will never leave the footsteps of his parents and will remain true under all circumstances to the principles of his religion. — Now I know you are in an association which I do not like and which awakens concern in me that you would like to abandon the ways of your parents."

The Assessor, who now saw where his uncle's talk was heading, defended himself and, since he well saw to whom the incrimination was applied, also defended the Doctor in every possible way. — But as the Dean did not want to listen and considered the Doctor to be a dangerous man, and declared him to be an atheist who was of no more worth than to be banished from Christendom, the Assessor became stirred up and spoke with decisive emphasis, "Doctor Wehrmann is a better Christian than any other that I know, and even you, my dearest uncle, are not excepted." — At this utterance the Dean turned vehement and said, "I do not want to be compared in any way with a man whom I despise and look on as a poisonous plant for human society." — The Assessor responded, "Best uncle, you go to far! — I have much to thank the Doctor, too much to thank him, than that I would calmly permit him to be disparaged in such a way." — The Dean seemed to brace himself, and spoke with a calm, but firm tone, "Nephew! You must give one up; me or the Doctor." — The Assessor wanted to speak, but the Dean interrupted him and said with vehemence, "Me or the Doctor." — "Come now, dear uncle," the Assessor now spoke solemnly, "stop your threatening and listen to my explanation. You believe, as you have often boasted about yourself, in the literal content of the Bible and you must for that reason have proven it. I will read to you the tests of a genuine Christian from the gospels, and if you are able to recognise them as true and are capable of factually proving them, then I want to ponder your words and see to what extent I can accept them. — Here are the tests." — He fetched the Bible, opened it at the gospel of Mark, and read the four well-known verses:

> Go ye into all the world, and preach the gospel to every creature.
> He that believeth and is baptized shall be saved; but he that believeth not shall be damned.
> And these signs shall follow them that believe; In my name shall they cast out devils; they shall speak with new tongues;

They shall take up serpents; and if they drink any deadly thing, it shall not hurt them; they shall lay hands on the sick, and they shall recover.

According to this, I declare solemnly that if you can demonstrate one of these tests as condition of faith, as condition of a true Christian, and the Doctor cannot, then I will give up my association with him. But should you not be able to, but the Doctor is capable of it, then I swear he shall remain my guide and teacher so long as I live."

"You are a fool," the Dean now cried, "who draws poison from secretive truths. — What mortal would now be capable of passing such tests which you could only pass in the first period of Christianity, in the vicinity of the saviour. — Our first Christian duty consists in recognising our incapacity, on the other hand to believe unconditionally in such works wherewith Christ and his apostles exalted themselves." — "I know enough," the Assessor now said. "In the gospels no time is given in which such works shall be accomplished. It states without any limitation: 'these signs shall follow them that believe'. — Anyone who wants to limit the sense of these words does no better than those who want to leave Christ entirely out of play in respect to religion. — The tests must be able to be passed now and forever, then Christianity has a reality. — In the other case, however, where you set aside such teaching which commands us to a positive action, to a factual delivery of proof, and declare it out of leisureliness to be unworkable, you deny, like the scribes and Pharisees, the Messiah, torture and crucify him, and will receive the reward of the scribes and Pharisees."

The Dean, when he saw the stubbornness of the Assessor, stood up, called out the window to his coachman and ordered him to get ready to depart as quickly as possible. — The Assessor was too agitated to be able to make an attempt to placate his uncle. — The Dean remained unmoved standing by the window in order to leave straightaway as soon as the coachman were to drive up. The latter gave the signal and the Dean left with the words, "You have me or the Doctor to give up. — If you have Christian sense, the choice is easy; if you don't have it, then I have also lost nothing." — He hurried quickly down the steps and climbed into the carriage. The Assessor accompanied him, despite his displeasure, to the carriage and called after him, as he drove away, a loud farewell. — His wife, who had heard the dispute of the men, let herself be seen again when the Dean had already departed. She asked her husband about the cause of the exchange of words. He placated her with the words, "My uncle required of me that I put aside my Christian confession of faith; but since this did not turn out entirely to his mind, he was peevish, wanted to instruct me, and when he did not succeed in this, he called the coachman and drove away extremely bitter."

His wife was satisfied because she was not particularly fond of the Dean on account of a certain apostolic severity. The Assessor, however, sought out the Deacon in order to give him news of this event.

***

Visit to the Doctor

The Assessor met the Deacon along the way, joined him straightaway, and informed him of the quarrel with the Dean, his uncle. They decided to visit the Doctor, and to tell him about the event in order to thereby receive perhaps more detailed information about the well-known tests of faith. They went to him, but met Professor Solbring there, with whom he seemed enveloped in a deep conversation. They wanted to leave again, but the Doctor called on them to stay, in that he said, "What the good Professor and I have to discuss, you may surely hear, since you are old acquaintances, and our discussion touches things which could likewise be of interest to you. The good Professor namely lies caught between belief and doubt and does not know on what side he should land. The four test verses of the gospel of Mark are for him so difficult to digest that he fears he might ruin his stomach forever by them. Perhaps you, my friends, also have a need for a few antacids, and there it is in one about whether one offers you only one or several straightaway. I therefore ask the good Professor to continue in his opposition. It concerns namely," he continued towards the other two, "the truth of the four verses which we established as the tests for Christianity." — The Professor began to talk and said, "I must confess, the four verses are of a sort that, if you read them only halfway with sound eyes, they cannot be interpreted; for the words: these signs shall follow them that believe, are the — allow, on account of their consequence and logical position, no other interpretation. Only, as soon as we look at the tests themselves, then anyone must confess that they are of a sort which exceeds all belief." — To this the Doctor responded, "Tests must be believed because you see with your eyes."

Professor: "Where do we find the tests?"

Doctor: "Have you ever sought such?"

Professor: "What use is seeking when you know in advance that nothing is to be found?"

Doctor: "With that sort of thinking, you will certainly never find something. No initiate delivers factual proof of hidden senses because, instead of believing, you would persecute him with envy and suspicion."

Professor: "Who could be so low?"

Doctor: "Everyone who would feel overwhelmed and did not have the strength to confess their error. — Humans can give up anything easier than they can give up a preconceived idea or a prejudice."

Professor: "Accordingly would the opposition lie not only in disbelief, but also in the unfortunate dogmatism of humans?"

Doctor: "I cannot deny it."

Professor: "And you do not consider me to be free of this weakness either?"

Doctor: "That you must yourself know best."

Professor: "I must confess that, irregardless that I treasure you highly before many others, I would have had a small pleasure in causing you an embarrassment."

Doctor: "And, in the case it should have succeeded with me to be victorious over this schadenfreude, would I have not then delivered a small test?"

Professor: "Perhaps through driving out devils?"

Doctor: "Call it what you will! But I must say as much that nobody who could not support themselves on factual proof would defeat their dogmatism."

Professor: "Driving out devils, talking with new tongues, dispelling snakes, drinking deadly poison without harm, and finally alleviating illness by the laying on of hands must not be initiated in that from such activities a mischief would arise where you would be at your wit's end with exorcists and miracle doctors."

Doctor: "Well, and you consider that the belief in such tests does not dominate among all peoples? — Then you know little of humanity. — Amongst the townsfolk, and especially in the countryside, this belief has such firm roots that it is not to be eradicated. But in that lies the saddening thing, that this belief is without teachers and guides. — The genteel folk and scholars are withdrawing from those regions, denying and abandoning in the comfort of self-cleverness the factual demonstration of the holiest matter of humanity to hysterically ill girls, gypsies, shepherds, hunters, sanctimonious idlers and a whole army of sybarites who have a great time at the expense of the blind and those led by no shepherd and who distance humanity ever further from the goal."

Professor: "In this I agree unconditionally. If tests are to be had, then it must be done by the first, by the most enlightened of a people, not though by the uneducated and the ignorant. — It is thus only about whether the tests are to be had at all."

Here a small pause occurred. — The Doctor seemed to be pondering, looked at the others and finally said, "The good Professor sets the knife to my throat and forces me to give up what I own; and therefore I say: the tests are to be had."

Professor: "Since you yourself say I am setting the knife to your throat, I want to use my momentary superiority and ask you: have you ever passed such tests?"

Doctor: "I saw this question coming and answer to it: that I would have to consider myself the most despicable of persons to get round such important things with lies and to claim something of which I would not have indisputable proof. I have not in my life paid an account without doing my sums. I would be ashamed to say I have climbed the Rigi if it had not occurred. Thus I tell you now, and reinforce it at the same time under oath, that I have not spoken a word in respect to religion and the original laws of it whose truth I have not previously found proved by practical experience."

Professor: "Thank you. Your word is to me a greater guarantee than all writings. But allow me one more question: what does it mean to speak with new tongues? — Orthodoxy considers it to be the ability to talk in all languages so that the German is able to speak Greek with the Greeks, Indian with the Indians, Chinese with the Chinese, in short with any inhabitant of the earth in the language of their land. — Does the meaning of the new tongues referred to lie in this?"

Doctor: "The essential thing in what is referred to as new tongues is actually the basic principle of the entire Bible and at the same time the means of passing the tests prescribed in the four verses. — The most sublime characteristic of humanity is language. But this must not only be awoken in the mouth, where it merely goes outward, but rather into all parts of the body, into all inner and outer organs, then the human knows what spiritual power and freedom is; then he will alleviate illnesses with his hand, drive out snakes, and set aside the danger of death."

The Professor looked at the Doctor with an astonished look, like a man who had fallen from the moon and told him of news from there. — Finally he said, "What you say is so surprising and new that one has trouble grasping it. You are claiming the most sublime characteristic of humanity is language. I want to attempt once to draw from this sentence a few consequences — the most sublime characteristic is language; language is words; words are light; light is life — the entire body possesses life, consequently it must also have light and words everywhere within it. — Provided that this conclusion contains reality, then the new tongues are grounded in the nature of the human and connect with his nature in such a way that it stops being a miracle, by comparison appearing to be the highest miracle of nature. — Good Doctor! If it is seriously about the awakening of the stated new tongues and not just a poetic phrase, then I ask you to release the tongues of all parts of my body, my inner and outer organs, and not spare me with any of the necessary operations."

Doctor: "Everybody must themselves carry out the operation on themselves; one cannot do anything but put the means in their hands. You have already received more of it, will receive still more, and then it is only about the firmness of your will to loosen the tongues, all or only a part, entirely or only halfway."

The Professor promised to do whatever was possible. The others also agreed to this promise and, as they left, took the conviction with themselves that the Doctor must have found the key to secrets of nature of which in our day you have no idea and no suspicion anymore.

***

Prophecy

The Professor, before he visited the Doctor again, invited the Assessor and the Deacon over a few times in order to speak with them about everything which he and they had heard from the Doctor, and to form by combining with them a plan or a sort of system.

The Assessor took this opportunity to repeat the story of Apollo and developed his thoughts over the value of an ideal realised in the story. Here everyone seemed to find their way somewhat; for to imitate an established exemplar lies so close to human nature that you often set too great a value on it and see in the agreement of insignificant trivialities with the exemplar great perfections. — Even the Professor felt himself drawn so much to cultivate himself in this way that he derived from it the most splendid connections and almost now considered himself a wise man.

The Deacon brought after this the Pestalozzian method into the discussion in that he made the claim that the most excellent exemplar did not suffice as long as you did not know the elements by which it had obtained its perfection. — Each endeavoured to speak about this spiritual doctrine of elements, but soon one felt like the next that they were only playing with phrases which bore in themselves no single trait of elemental characteristics. "Here we are not competent enough," the Professor finally said; "you as much as I, and I as much as you. Here only the Doctor can shed light. No book, no school, no university, and no doctrine known to me is capable of it. Only the Doctor alone; yes, I would like to say — he alone amongst all the inhabitants of the earth."

After they had struggled in vain to find something elemental, the simple method of the carpenters was raised, which surprised the Professor and gave him opportunity to express himself quite aptly over it.

"It is," he said, "a capability in the human by means of which he can himself comprehend and know. How far this capability reaches and where it ends, to know this seems to be the keystone to the teaching of the Doctor, the keystone to all doctrines of wisdom. — The ancients spoke so much about an unbridled genius that you will often be tempted as a layperson to believe they were speaking of a human characteristic which was previously bound, but then unleashed produced an Iliad, called into life the artworks of a Phidias*, a Pausanias†, an Apollo, and many others. — Who can give us information about it? — Answer: amongst all mortals only the Doctor. We will go to him, in the mood in which we find ourselves, ask him whether there is such a genius, in what connection the new tongues stand to it; and whether it is possible finally for mortals to approach the innermost sanctum of God and nature in such a way that the puzzle of life is solved by it and immortality becomes a necessary consequence of its existence. — But I will say one thing on him: I will do all violence in the presence of the Doctor to not get carried away by his superiority, so that we come to the most evident conviction of whether he too, self-conscious of his error, has erected a firm structure and not just a magnificent show facade."

They went together to the Doctor and found him alone, reclining on the sofa. They apologised in case they had disturbed his midday rest. He rose quickly and said, "It was no rest in which you found me. I was exercising a little in the handling of my new tongues in order to obtain, even if not a virtuosity, a not entirely common dexterity. — You are heartily welcome to be here, and please take a seat."

After they had sat down, the Professor said, "Good Doctor, I have already noticed one must prepare oneself to always be surprised by your answers. You speak of the new tongues like of a matter which can be put entirely at our command, indeed so that the new tongues relate to one's free will like the register of an organ to the will of the organist who can open and then close them again as he wishes. — What sort of capability is that then? And with what name is it described in everyday life?"

Doctor: "In everyday life it has various names. — Christians call it rebirth, Christ too, but mostly the holy spirit.

---

* [Tr.: 5th century BCE Athenian sculptor.]
† [Tr.: 2nd century CE Greek geographer and historian.]

Muslims recognise it in the voice of the prophets. — To the Brahmans it is the heavenly wisdom; to the Jews the word of God; according to the concepts of our time we must call it prophesy."

Professor: "What is prophesy?"

Doctor: "The power which sees into the hidden, connects time with eternity, ties past and future to the present, and looks through with spiritual vision; it is the living light of all knowledge and ability; it penetrates everything, animates everything, and delivers us the proof of immortality."

Professor: "Who is called to prophecy?"

Doctor: "All humanity, for it is a gift of our nature."

Professor: "If it were such a gift, it would also have to be known in our time when one seeks and uses all the powers of nature."

Doctor: "It would be known too, if a great part of humanity did not bristle against it."

Professor: "Who bristles against it?"

Doctor: "You and all of your mind who seem to fear the voice of a positive truth before which the self-cleverness would have to vanish."

Professor: "But do you consider, to the extent such a gift were present and was developed, what confusion would have to arise from it? — Each would pretend to be a prophet and delude his neighbour today with this and tomorrow with that, and in this way spread hate and discord, fantasy and superstition."

Doctor: "How short-sightedly people whom you must count amongst the rational ones gaze at the world. — What mischief has the ability to make fire already caused? Should it therefore not be present? — What horror and desolation has occurred through gunpowder? And yet it would not occur to any rational person to wish it had not been discovered. — What evil have books already brought about, how many hearts poisoned, and how many false principles spread? — Should there therefore be no scholars, no books anymore which by the uses which they provide humanity make good again the evil a thousand times over? Thus it goes when the most splendid artistic gift of humanity, prophesy, awakes again and is brought into practice where some error could take place and some misuse could occur; but what would that be against the benefits of a free knowledge drawn from within yourself, whereby philosophy would again obtain a foothold, the word "wisdom" would obtain meaning, and even religion would be lifted to a standpoint where you could sit in dialogue with God, the spirit of Christ, and could inquire into all the spiritual secrets of nature. — Truly I say, anyone to whom such a state does not appear worth wishing for is like a vandal for whom in the sculpture of a Phidias the stone has more value than the sculpture itself. — Indeed, anyone who does not see in such a state the happiness of the world has no free thoughts and clings to the dust where he can think and feel nothing holy."

Professor: "I must confess, the good Doctor does not crack the whip badly when it comes to driving out a devil. Only I thank him and ask him whenever an unclean rabble stirs in me to always proceed in a similar way. Only I allow myself still the question whether history does not grant us evidence of the development of such gifts residing in all humanity."

Doctor: "The Israelites and all primitive peoples had prophets; from where could they have drawn this art other than from themselves? For to assume God had decided before the appearance of each of these prophets to now once more make a prophet means to sin against the spirit of nature, against the spirit of humanity, and against the spirit of justness of God which favours nobody with its gifts, but rather gives to everybody everything which leads them to freedom and to the determination of life.

The Israelites had schools of prophets. All thorough historical researchers and theologians testify that Elias headed such a one. — The Bible itself speaks of children of the prophets. What sort of children could they have been? — But certainly none other than such men who were members of the schools of prophets and themselves attended them. — If we consider the history of Persia and India only somewhat with an open mind, then we bump into numerous things which are not to be comprehended without such a spiritual clarity. — Over the Greek mysteries and oracles much is fabled, but of the matter and its nature no rational words have been spoken. It may be that with such institutions mistakes occur; but are you therefore permitted to damn an institution when not all the students of it achieve the prescribed goal? — Enough, prophecy definitely existed with the ancients. — Why should we not also still have what they possessed? — Why should we, in a period when all the sciences stand so high, be ignorant about the most important point of life, about the most splendid gift of humanity?"

To the Deacon these discussions, as they belonged to his subject, were especially important. Thus he entered the conversation and said, "If prophecy is a gift of human nature and with it the noted tests of Christianity can be passed, then it is religion itself, and the confessions to one religion or another are superfluous."

Doctor: "Since the Christian religion is nothing more and nothing less than a school of prophets, the Christian religion can at the least dispense with everything else. Whether other religions also seek and fulfil this aim is not something to be discussed here, since we are only concerned with the Christian religion here. — Certainly we see few fruits of this school, see no children of the prophets and no prophets anymore; only the school, the Christian religion is not at fault for that, but rather our perverse minds, our prejudices, by means of which we think the aim of our religious life is fulfilled by the reading of the old prophecies. — Is that not directly so, as if you wanted to sing no other musical melodies than those David made for his psalms? — For three thousand years Christianity was announced and prepared for by prophecy, and finally founded by the most sublime prophecy, and even spread by it amongst the peoples. Now it is asked: can Christianity, which was prepared through prophecy, founded and spread by it, be surely nourished and reproduced in any other way than by prophecy? — No industry, no art, and no science can continue to exist if you do not carry it on. But once a matter is forgotten, then stories, moral references, and pious wishes are of no help. — You must then climb down into yourself, must clean out the buried shaft of your inner being and, like a primitive son, take nature as your teacher, and in the exploration of its words lift the lost to the light of day again. — Thus it is for us with Christianity; its spirit has been lost and no means remains to us but to seek within ourselves to awaken there the mediator and have ourselves taught buy it. — Christ is this mediator. He is the representative of a prophecy placed eternally in humanity, indeed, he is even prophecy itself because he could only be through it, be then before Abraham was, and will be in all eternity."

Here the Doctor fell silent. — To the three listeners, the idea prophecy is a natural gift placed in every human was so new that they could have easily been doubtful here if it had been possible for them to put the Doctor's words in doubt. They confessed to the Doctor openly their thoughts and asked him to speak about this subject often and a lot so that they could become accustomed to it and think about it without inhibition.

***

The Rural Excursion

Since the Professor had heard from the Doctor so many things which he could not work out with all his acumen, the old urge to doubt returned and took from him the uninhibitedness of his free thinking. In such a mood he spoke to himself, "We only ever see the Doctor in his apartment. — We are the visitors, he is the host. — We come as students and he is the teacher. In this position he already has the predominance which he impresses us with. I must bring him into a situation where he is our equal; where the impressions of the day and the circumstances affect him just as they affect us; if he maintains his superiority and dignity there, then I must believe that an inner, infallible power guides him and I can adhere to him with more unconditional faith." — To this end he decided to stage an outing into the countryside, to invite the Doctor and both his friends, and to pay attention to the former so precisely that not even the smallest unsoundness and ambiguity would escape him. He immediately made the preparations, invited all three personally, and since nobody gave him a negative answer, he drove on the specified day, in the morning at nine o'clock, with a comfortable carriage to the Doctor in order to pick up all three participants there.

It was Sunday. The sky had brightened after a thundershower in the night and poured its light as if in triumph on the refreshed fields. The Doctor, whose disposition was extremely receptive for the impressions of nature, felt in the most cheerful mood and unfurled along the way an abundance of life views so that the Professor often forgot he was today called not just for pleasure, but for critique. The Doctor, although he seemed to suspect as much, did not allow himself to be disturbed in the stream of his questions and answers, his parables and remarks, so that everyone, put into the most comfortable of moods, experienced the journey of two miles like a short walk through a park. The Professor had ordered everything in advance, even a breakfast for restoration after the journey. This was taken and then it was decided to stroll about for a time in the place in order to see the Sunday demeanours of the inhabitants and at the same time see the local facilities. — Here too the Doctor played the main role; for it was no less than as if he had been born here or had been acquainted with the people for years already, so trustingly did he know to greet them, speak with them, and make remarks about all the circumstances of their lives. — The Professor, who also felt the superiority of the Doctor here, said to his two companions as the Doctor was directly surrounded by an entire circle of residents and speaking with them in the most good-natured of moods, "Is it not as if the Doctor were our lord and we his servants." — The Deacon replied, "I think it is as if he were the teacher and we the students whom he, in order to make it a good day for them, leads on a stroll in the countryside." — The Doctor stepped out of the circle, joined his companions, and suggested that now might surely be time for lunch. — To the Professor the ease of the behaviour and the unfeigned joy of the Doctor were so conspicuous that he several times felt embarrassed and could not foresee anymore how he would bring him onto another subject than the beauties and joys of the day.

They returned to the tavern. The meal was carried out and to everyone it seemed, despite the small breakfast which they had taken on arriving, stirred up by the strolling about the place and the cheerful discourse, to taste excellent. The wine too, which the Professor had ordered especially for the carrying out of his intention, was quite strongly partaken of so that he began quite confidently to calculate on catching the Doctor in some sort of weakness. But he had calculated in vain, for the Doctor became during the meal more and more in the mood, so that by and by everything, even the most insignificant objects, received a sort of consecration. Of course the conversation, after the dessert had been brought out and the servants had been gone for some time, led to religion and to everything which they had previously heard, doubted, and then believed again. Amongst these topics prophecy seemed to emerge as the main theme in order to be illuminated from all sides. — After the Assessor, the Deacon, and also the Professor had expressed themselves over this marvellous gift of

The Rural Excursion

the creator on which all religions rested, the Doctor entered the conversation and gave the following lecture.

"The common man desires prophecy because he sees no salvation at all for the future without it; and if the Parson cannot give him it, then he goes to gypsies, hunters, and shepherds. The countryman wants to see with his eyes, wants to perceive physically in order to be able to believe spiritually. We therefore call him simple-minded and superstitious because he desires a proof of that which has been preached to him from youth on. I consider that to desire a proof for something which you are taught and imposed on as necessary is nothing less than simple-minded, in contrast to the only correct process approved by reason. — The scholars indeed are of another view and claim the extrasensory is never to be proved. The simple human mind must say to this: then there is also nothing extrasensory. As simple-mindedly and unanswerably true as this sentence is, it is though not listened to and acknowledged, to the contrary it is shouted down as nonsense and lack of intelligence because you enjoy yourself far better on a throne of hypotheses where you cannot be touched, cannot be understood, and so feel entitled to practise the dictatorship in comfortable certainty and darkness. — The countryman desires proof; the bold rational person desires it just as much; we belong amongst them and therefore want to see from which sources we might draw something positive.

In former times, in order to find proof of a spiritual life, you sought after gnomes, fairies, witches, and kobolds. Spirits and ghosts reign in our times just as much as previously. — Indeed, I maintain amongst thousands of houses or even families, both in the cities and in the countryside, you will encounter not one house or one family where the belief in spirits and ghosts does not reign as the foundation for the belief in immortality. The noble and disbelieving demeanour which you see amongst the so-called educated proves nothing but that you can make it — to speak against your feeling and your conviction — also into a passing fashion. There are indeed a few who deny and reproach everything, but these stick the genius of life so firmly in raw flesh tat they also do not feel the least trace of having ever felt it. These indeed call themselves the rational, the philosophers, and the lights of the age; but I do not know under which class of creatures to put them; whether amongst humans, or merely monsters gifted with human faces. — The true human wants to be immortal, but desires proof for it.

We have spoken of a sort of proof which is worth more to humans than astute demonstrations. — But it is also true, to the extent you could see a dead person wander about as a ghost, that would certainly deliver a more evident proof than all the libraries on earth. But since the wandering about as ghost is not appropriately established and is challenged by many, and indeed not without good reason, you are intent at all times on seeking other, more general means of proof accessible to every human being and, in order to preserve them for humanity more securely, establishing them as positive laws. — In this striving we find the basic cause of all religions of the earth, both of ancient and modern times. — What sort of means of proof are they though? — Answer: the art of gazing into yourself, awakening your inner being to a free spiritual activity, drawing out the most perfect purest spirit of human nature from flesh and blood in order by means of it to become convinced by an innate, royal self-knowledge.

Self-knowledge! To the schoolteacher an inexplicable, incomprehensible word, because he considers that you can obtain positive knowledge only in the school and from books. But he forgets thereby that the rough primitive man can count just as certainly to five as the most senior accountant. — The genius of humanity drawn from flesh and blood does not need to learn anything; the natural human, however, needs the school. The inner genius indeed uses this school too in order to connect itself closer to the natural human and to make itself more understandable to him, but by nature it is as free as the creator himself. — With what names, however, will we have to describe the revelations which the natural human receives from the genius or the spirit. As so many varied names are already used, I know none better for my manner of explanation than — prophecy.

Only now we can ask: what is prophecy? And give the answer: prophecy is the revelation of the awoken spirit or genius which it shares with the externally sensory human. — Under which conditions does this genius reveal itself? — It reveals itself to us when we put aside everything we have learnt, heard, and preserved in memory, free ourselves of all that to which temporal desires entice us, vanquish impulsiveness and passions, and thus give the inner life space to stir and move itself at its pleasure and teach us through sensations, words, and sights. — Expressed here is the nature of prophecy from its smallest sphere of activity to its greatest extent, where past and future are mirrored in the present. — Here we catch sight of the elementary basis and grounds on which we can build according to the measure of our natural gifts. — Here we are shown the possibility of realising the highest ideal of humanity, like Christ. — Here we also come to the position of the carpenters, who set about those who do not comprehend it with every possible nickname, but once comprehended it is no different than if had come with us into the world and we can no longer imagine anymore at all the state when we did not comprehend it.

Indeed one says: if this power were innate to the human and a gift of his nature, why do we see so little proof of its presence? — Here it must be answered: Everything great and distinguished is rare; but we find the mediocre in every field numerous. — World history has only one Homer, but each age teems with poets and rhymesters. And yet it is true that only those who try their hand at the art of poetry are in a position to evaluate the greatness of Homer; to the others the Iliad is a book which contains a few curious stories which you could have heard just as well in a tavern. It is so and no different in the realm of prophecy. — Ancient history provides us with four great prophets; the average, however, follow the most recent model, against whom the earlier ones were only small lights. Christ is the hero of this sublime art who stands like a column of light in the history of the world and illuminates prehistory and posterity. — To the extent now it is true that nobody who has tried their hand at the art of poetry is capable of recognising the magnificence of Homer, we may conclude all the more certainly that nobody is in a position to evaluate the prophecy of Christ who has not awoken their spirit in themself and penetrated into the sanctum of this art, even if only weakly. But anyone who has found the spirit of prophecy even in only the slightest degree in themself will, like the little poet towards Homer, know as well to recognise and evaluate the sublimeness of the founder of the Christian religion. —

You should not believe that prophecy belongs to the area of impossibility because we are incapable of explaining it. Can we demonstrate the power of sight? — Do we know with what we measure the relationship of notes and their chords? — Has anyone ever discussed with what power he can transfer himself in thought into the past, into the future, and into other parts of the world? We possess these attributes, and to know that we possess them is all we are capable of. So prophecy as a gift of humanity is a power whose presence we only have to seek; to desire further explanations means to enter a labyrinth from which we would never discover the way out. — The liberated genius in us is the prophet, the knowledge of it is our highest knowledge. But now it is to be asked: what shall or what can this prophet reveal to us? — The answer is: it reveals to us at first its existence. Through this revelation we are put in a position to recognise the divine in human nature. Then it reveals to us that it is destined to connect itself with the natural ego of the human in order to guide it with itself to immortality. It reveals to us the secrets of God and his word, which has made everything from which it itself arises and therefore bears infallibility, like God himself, within itself. It reveals to us that it stands above time, has no yesterday and no tomorrow, but rather flowed around by eternity can only gaze, hear, think, and feel in it. — It reveals to us what we wish and desire in respect to our destiny, in respect to God and eternity, in that it guides us to the original source of life from which we see all of its turnings and circumstances in their necessity and subordinate ourselves to its laws in good spirit.

True prophecy, however, is not only a knowledge of otherwise hidden things, but also an ability, an accomplishment. Anyone who possesses just a mustard seed of pure prophecy can lay their hands on the sick and it will become better with them. They will drive out snakes and take the poison from fatal drinks. They will be capable of everything and possess what belongs to the tests of the Christian, I would like to say of the tests of humanity. — And so I close this lecture with the remark: anyone here who does not believe is against themselves and the spirit of nature and cannot make any claims on a reward; but anyone who believes and draws the pure genius of the highest knowledge from his flesh will feast on the pleasures of life and not be able to comprehend how it is possible to live in any other way."

Since the Doctor fell silent, the Assessor thus took the opportunity to speak and expressed himself in the following way: "Our enlightened friend and patron has unveiled such sublime views in his lecture over prophecy that you must be astonished about it. According to these remarks prophecy stands at a position where the dust and world of desires does not touch it and only the light of heaven and the purest classicism arises from it. In this way it is a matter which could only be realised through the most perfect ideal, through Christ. — Prophecy is the eternal Christ who already was before there was Abraham and will be until the end of all days. — If ever an idea could clarify just the nature of Christianity, then it is this, where I see our religion not bound to a personality or a time, but rather must consider it to be a product of an eternal light without beginning."

The Deacon now entered the conversation and said, "I would have to speak against my convictions if I did not want to share my friend Selbach's views. Only, I do not consider the good Doctor's lecture so complete as he finds it. — We know now what prophecy is, but we do not yet know whatever the means is to obtain it. To direct oneself to an exemplar may be morally good, but we do not yet know the elements with which one, like Raphael with the paintbrush, should practise daily. — Even the method of the master carpenter, where you learn to comprehend through the practice of the matter, cannot come into use because we see no test of Christianity amongst the millions of practising Christians. The good Doctor has already spoken earlier about schools of prophets. He knows this school, otherwise he would not have spoken about it. Surely he will take us into the school so that we, like a primary school student, will go from counting to calculating and from the ABC to reading and spelling." — The other two agreed with this wish and the Doctor responded.

"With all the mysteries of ancient and modern times, the ones entering, in order to testify to their earnestness, had to subject themselves to specific examinations. In our days they not only mock these examinations, but even the mysteries themselves. — However anyone may consider it here, I consider examinations to be expedient because they give a warranty that you will not be scared away by the strange manner of the learning method. — I will also apply an examination to you which may perhaps be more difficult that the instruction itself. The examination consists of the following.

Assume the presence of prophecy as a natural gift of humanity only to be an hypothesis, then read the Bible and give me, supported on that hypothesis, the proof that all the apparently supernatural miracles of that book are to be explained philosophically by it, and I will present to you in order the system of a school of prophets. — But so as to protect you from any error, I will add that you have to consider all the images and phenomena of the Bible not objectively, but subjectively. The images and words which the prophets saw and heard came down to them neither from heaven, nor from an entity external to them. Everything was given to them by their own, internally resident spirit which forms, creates, and speaks a ray of God, like God himself, uninterruptedly, and thereby reveals the secrets of time and eternity. To begin with we get to know only small sparks of this spirit; these become candles, finally stars in whose brilliance we view ourselves. — When we now stay persistent, when we seek to get ever closer to it, then it reveals to us its workshop, lets us take part in its works, and raises us finally to the rewards of persistence — to a mastery where we are making the decisions ourselves and performing in its place."

The Professor, who despite his attentiveness had up to then maintained a sort of observant calm, was surprised by the final words in such a way that he forgot his role and burst out in the following utterance: "What the good Doctor has just said is so new and great that no common power of thought could be in a position to invent it. I have heard and read much, but nothing similar. Here prophecy is in play; here new tongues are speaking; for a common tongue would hardly be capable of reading it out. — The good Doctor has delivered today the most difficult of all tests which can serve us as a sign of whether one is a Christian, in a word, whether one is a complete human. I pay homage to him with the most sincere veneration of my heart, will seek to pass the imposed examination and ask him then also to teach me to speak with new tongues."

The others joined in the promise and in the request of the Professor, and appraised the present day as being the most important of their lives.

The Doctor understood the art of drawing the appropriate use from this mood in that he, instead of raising the exaltation, declared that one should surely keep such moments in memory, but the fire which penetrates our demeanours in such a mood must be allowed to spread calmly so that it does not become a blazing flame and consume itself.

Some more yet was spoken about less important topics which probably deserves to be recorded, but will be passed over in order not to be too rambling. — Enough, the small company remained together in a refreshing mood for so long that they only got home late and parted with the assurances of indissoluble friendship.

***

The Bible

The Assessor and the Deacon had long since read the Bible according to the Doctor's instructions and awaited the fulfillment of his promise. But the latter hesitated in the hope the Professor would also have soon passed his examination. — Since they suspected the cause, they adapted themselves to this delay and were therefore very pleased when the Professor said to them one day that he had read the Bible and hoped the Doctor would be content with him. They arranged the time of the visit with him and arrived a few days later to receive from him the information on the promised means of awakening prophecy in themselves. — The Doctor said, as they entered, "It seems you want to besiege me and force me to pay the promised contribution. Here no force is needed. If you have fulfilled the conditions, then I must not leave my own unfulfilled. I therefore ask you in all formality to provide a report to me and to convince me of the success of your examinations." —

The Assessor started first and said, "To the extent prophecy is present in human nature as a gift, we can consider the phenomenon of extraordinary prophets in the same way as is done in the subjects of others arts and sciences with distinguished geniuses. Unusual gifts, circumstances of time, and diligence produce the powers of the spirit, and new and unusual things appear. According to this way of reading the Bible, it is a psychology for humanity which could not be more apt, because we find in it examples of all degrees and for all the circumstances of life."

The Deacon filed his report as follows: "As a clergyman I was obligated not only to read the Bible, but to study it. This study did indeed not bear the fruits I was expecting because I did not know how to reconcile the phenomena and divinations contained therein with the course of nature and the gifts of humanity. But if prophecy in all its branches is a gift of human nature, then the Bible is a book which only describes the incidents of world history which arose from spiritual powers and can only be comprehended by means of them."

The Professor, for whom, despite his good will, it was still as if he found himself in a land whose language he did not understand, presented his report thus: "It is true, if humans possess prophetic powers, then in the Bible much becomes clear and natural which without such a gift would not be in a state to be explained. But many places are not to be interpreted without the direct influence of God. When the prophet Micaiah in the book of Kings 22:19–22 says:

> I saw the Lord sitting on his throne, and all the host of heaven standing by him on his right hand and on his left.
> And the Lord said, Who shall persuade Ahab, that he may go up and fall at Ramothgilead? And one said on this manner, and another said on that manner.
> And there came forth a spirit, and stood before the Lord, and said, I will persuade him.
> And the Lord said unto him, Wherewith? And he said, I will go forth, and I will be a lying spirit in the mouth of all his prophets. And he said, Thou shalt persuade him, and prevail also: go forth, and do so.

Here the subjectivity stops and God himself makes use of an arbitrary dictatorship in that he says, I want it so, so do it."

The Doctor replied, "You are right. God makes use here of dictatorship and seems to say, I want it so. — But how can we imagine in a more rational way that the divinity which looks around and fills the universe has left all the other lands and peoples in the lurch and is holding before Micaiah's eyes an advisory council with all the heavenly host in order to find a false spirit which will turn the heads of the sycophantic prophets of Ahab? Someone who imagines such a thing in seriousness proves that he stands on the lowest step of thinking and does not yet possess the power to gaze into the mirror of truth. — What Micaiah saw was admittedly God, but that God which resides in him; that part of the immeasurable whole which collects in his inner being and draws the future in prophetic images. It is therefore the purest subjectivity when at the command of God he prophesies downfall to the

The Bible

king Ahab. — We must consider all the phenomena in the Bible in this way, and if we are drawn by the strangeness of the words and images almost by force to objectivity, then we shall not be led astray and shall await the point in time when it must become clear to us."

The Assessor, who was entirely clear on this point, nevertheless made the remark that the phenomenon of Christ must be considered to be an objective thing, to be a phenomenon external to us.

The Professor quickly grasped this idea and said, "Christ is brought into no such subjectivity where we are not required to seek outside ourselves and to receive instruction from an individual."

The other two looked with these words at the Doctor to see whether he was not perhaps embarrassed by such remarks. He kept his composure and broke down his views over the objective and subjective Christ in the following way.

"The personality of Christ is objective, his spirit though is subjective. Without the spirit the personality possesses no worth. Christ himself said about it: my flesh and blood is no use, but my words are spirit and life*. — He clears up for us with these few words the relationship of objectivity and subjectivity completely. The more we worry about his personality, the less his spirit becomes clear to us. The more we recognise his spirit, however, the more beneficially his personality affects us in that it becomes an ideal and exemplar to us, also enters into us and forms us according to him. — The personality is the bearer of the spirit and in this respect is of importance. But anyone who forget the treasure because of the bearer is not worthy of the treasure. — We see in our time where the historical struggle over the personality of Christ leads and has already led: to unbelief, to dogma, to sectarianism, to speciality and to contentiousness, which all are losing together in small-minded pettiness the sense for the eternal and the divine, and gifting for it their attentiveness to the flesh and blood and for an epoch."

---

* [Tr.: cf. John 6:63: It is the spirit that quickeneth; the flesh profiteth nothing: the words that I speak unto you, they are spirit, and they are life.]

The Professor responded to this lecture, "The correct view of this double Christ seems to be absolutely the point which many people do not focus on enough and hence then stumble and, to the extent they do not make the effort to again stand firm, finally fall."

The Doctor replied, "It is the cliff to which already many have pushed themselves and made themselves incompetent for the entire time of their life. — To make the word of God alive in yourself is the teaching, is the spirit of Christ. The prophets spoke through the word of God and announced Christianity. But he is the most sublime prophet, the most glorious bearer of the word of God, and therefore because of this word an exemplar to us. — It is the word, however, which makes us Christians. Indeed, if we could magic his person down from heaven, we would obtain nothing by it so long as we did not hear his words in us. — A war of annihilation was carried out about the fame of where Homer was given birth to. What did the art of poetry obtain thereby? Certainly nothing at all; to the contrary, Homer's remembrance was profaned by it. Had his supposed countrymen studied the spirit of his unsurpassable poems, they they would have served a glorious matter. It was just the same in reference to the person and the spirit of Christ. — Let us seek his spirit, have his word made alive in us, then the prophecy, by means of which he called our divine religion to life, will come to us again and we will learn to praise and venerate his name through it."

This lecture seemed to have vanquished all doubt, for nobody said anything about it. — In taking their leave, however, they thanked the Doctor for the ever new instruction and images with which he was stilling their thirst for pure knowledge.

***

Wisdom

The Professor, regardless of still being plagued quite often by doubts, felt the urge in himself to break through all the veils and to penetrate into the sanctum of truth. To this end he arranged with his friends to visit the Doctor again, the sooner the better, and to move him to finally give them the means of revealing their inner being and recognising the spirit in complete clarity. He shared his wish and decided to remind the Doctor on his next visit of his word and to ask for the fulfillment of it. Thus it happened too; when they had assembled once more after about eight days again at his place, they came out with their request. The Doctor thought to himself for a few moments and began: "We have already spoken so much over one and the same object that you would believe the matter were exhausted and nothing new could be found in it anymore. Nevertheless I see though that, in order to satisfy your wish completely, we must admit ourselves into a relation in order to clarify the matter which it is about.

We have previously made use of the word 'prophecy'. As descriptive as this expression might also be, it is though subject to many misinterpretations in order to be able to use it for all branches of human knowledge and activity. We think, when prophecy is spoken of, that it could refer to nothing else but seeing into the future. — Prophecy comprises in an expanded sense everything where we *ourselves* know something, where we as it were drew and judged our views from an inner feeling. — In this general sense the word 'prophecy' does not find anymore the appropriate favour and therefore instead of it you make use of the word 'wisdom'.

What is wisdom is asked so often, but scholars and the unscholarly owe a satisfying answer. — Wisdom is, like prophecy, the light of the innate knowledge drawn from oneself which is given to us by the creator.

Apollo taught the shepherds music, that is, he placed the music into the soul of the countryman as well as into the souls of the townsfolk. It is just the same with wisdom, whose spark glows in every human being, from the beggar to the king. — Only wisdom is of a dual nature — sometimes worldly and other times divine.

Each human has an innate knowledge. Anyone who is clearly conscious of it and translates it into their life activity and professional business will, where they are active, perform sound things; those by contrast who do not know any of their innate knowledge will, whatever they undertake, not reach their goal. — We see humans who have studied the laws of their profession most meticulously and yet always remain wet behind the ears. Others barely look at the laws and guess with an inner instinct at the spirit of them. From this the good business people, upright officials, soldiers, leaders, in short all those carrying the bourgeois society in their hearts who exercise their legal duties, proceed without constantly looking up the written law. Others live for the dead letters of the law, are themselves dead and cold, and daily injure with every fulfillment of the law the spirit of the law. — It just the same in relation to morality. Anyone who does not carry it in their heart cannot be taught about it by any book or school. This self-knowledge and self-recognition is the first degree of wisdom which we see in the house arrangements of the countryman as well as in a large state's housekeeping.

We see another kind of inborn spiritual power in the sphere of art, where quite often artistic production appears of which the artist themselves, when it is completed, cannot give an account anymore of how it arose. This capability is in common life described by the terms "rapture" or "genius", which glows throughs the artist and makes him capable of ever new creations*. — The high character extracts from the artist, whereas the work, the visibleness in which it works spiritually and ethereally on the understanding and disposition, leads the paintbrush of the painter, the chisel of the sculptor, and the pen of the poet, and makes the harmonies of the spheres sound in the soul of the musician. — The human is great through this splendid capability. He releases himself from the dust, and if he does not have to hand over his artwork to the

---

* [Tr.: it is worth noting here that the German word for creation, *Schöpfung*, is derived from *schöpfen*, which means to scoop up or to draw (as in water), and so already holds within it the connotation of being drawn from some source.]

world, to fashion, and to extravagance, then the art could serve for a temple in which heavenly light illuminates and leads the artist to eternity. Only the latter does not yet obtain the laurels which he has flattered himself to receive. The power awoken in him can serve, however, to make him attentive to a purer genius which rises above time.

The highest characteristic of human nature is the divine wisdom where those born in dust free themselves from the dust and, creating the forms of eternity, themselves enter into eternity. — Here is the zenith of creation. — The god-born, inner human enters into effectiveness and fills our disposition not only with intuitions, but with words and feelings of an eternal life which everyone who struggles for must become part of.

This last act of wisdom must be sought after by anyone who wants to learn to recognise what it is to be a true Christian. — Here sentimental sayings, gestures, and feelings do not suffice. The word must come alive throughout our entire body, from the mouth to the toes and from the heels to the highest point of the skull.

Should I say still more? — Oh, that I may speak! — But it is better to say too little than too much; therefore each figure out from the little I will now say as much as he is capable.

Anyone who does not become one like this little child cannot enter into heaven*. — What is the first business of the little child? — Answer: that they learn to speak, at first letters, then syllables, then words. — Each proceed with his inner being just so.

Anyone who then denies that Christ came in the flesh is an antichrist. — The words of Christ are spirit and life. The spirit and the life have no special place in the body. They are spread throughout the entire body and reside in the flesh. — Hallow the flesh, draw the spirit out with the activity of the little child, then Christ has arisen in you.

Anyone who is not reborn in the spirit cannot enter into the kingdom of heaven†. — The matter is not to be expressed and written more clearly. — Hence become little children, do

---

*   [Tr.: cf. Matthew 18:4.]
†   [Tr.: cf. Matthew 18:3.]

what was said before, and the rebirth must follow, as truly as the grape becomes ripe with constant sunlight."

The Doctor spoke these words as if to himself, and now continued, "Consider what I have just said, then I will assist where it isn't working."

Those present had listened with eager attention to this almost oracular instruction and sought, in order to impress the memory on themselves, to repeat and even write it down word for word. They directed many more questions to the Doctor, but he answered evasively and declared that he had said enough. "Had I," he continued in his refusal, "heard such intimations, I would have arrived far sooner at the goal. But anyone who knows everything without possessing it satisfies himself in the end with the knowing and no riches are received. — Consider what I have said — word for word; let the practice follow the consideration and the spirit will certainly be awoken."

To the Professor it was as if he found himself in a different world where the human form had taken an entirely different direction. — The Assessor sought in vain for an ideal point on which he could tie his investigations. — But the Deacon said, "For me a light has turned on. — So if you do not become like one of these little children, you cannot enter into the heavenly realm is to me now such a clear sentence that it is to me like with the carpenters who cannot imagine how they ever could have not comprehended the use of the diagonal cross. — We must learn to speak, at first letters, then syllables and words, and finally entire sentences. — Only now do I comprehend the story of the great Chinese emperor Iao* who, in order to give the land good fortune, chose a fellow regent from the people. Iao is the root of the word, is God†; the fellow regent, however, is the mortal ruler chosen by God. — Only now do I see why to the later disciples of John the Baptist, the Gnostics or Neoplatonists these three letters were so important. — My dear good Doctor! Through your last intimations you have shown me the way to the elements of the word or of wisdom

---

*   [Tr.: possibly a reference to the legendary emperor Yao.]
†   [Tr.: Ἰαω (Iao) was often used by Hellenistic Jews for the tetragrammaton YHWH prior to the Christian era. It also refers to one of the Archons in Sethian Gnosticism.]

which I will use and in a short time arrive at a system like the Pestalozzian, to be able to work and reach the goal of my desires."

The others asked him and urged for explanations; but he said, "As soon as I have passed the test, I will explain myself; until then each is to seek themselves and then rejoice in the self-overcoming."

Since neither the Doctor, nor the Deacon was to be brought into further discussion, they parted, firmly resolved to use what had been heard that day as a foundation to safely build upon.

***

The Liaison

The Doctor had meanwhile, when his friends were not visiting him, had a small adventure which did not remain entirely without consequences in that it put him in contact with the clergy where he was required to also expose to them his theological views. He in fact encountered the uncle of the Assessor, the Dean mentioned above, in company where he did not at first know him, but later, when both had become acquainted, came up quite fiercely against one another and finally, according to the strict traditions of the duel, challenged each other to written presentation of the argument. — The matter proceeded as follows.

The Doctor had known already for some time the Parson Punter at O...b, and had already often promised to visit him in order to also see him in his parish. — It was a beautiful day and he decided to fulfil his promise without announcing his arrival beforehand. The Parson had great joy in seeing him there, but regretted at the same time not being able to dedicate the present day entirely to him, as the Dean had been invited with a few neighbouring clergy to lunch. — The Doctor wanted to go away again, only the Parson made him stay with the remark that such a Doctor as he would not be a dishonour to a company of clergy. He stayed, discussed various subjects with the Parson, then before lunch walked around the village for about an hour, and returned when he thought the time was right to the parsonage where the expected guests had already arrived. — The Doctor was introduced to the clergymen. The Dean, however, who had been occupied immediately beforehand in a conversation that was important to him, felt unpleasantly interrupted and hence did not pay any attention at all to the introduction of a Doctor whose chest was not adorned by at least *one* service decoration. Enough, he ignored the name Wehrmann and took the seat of honour when the soup arrived. — The courses were good, the wine no less so, and thus the company felt extremely edified.

After the meal was almost over, one of the clergymen present asked the Dean about the Assessor Selbach to whom he wished to assign some business. The Dean replied that he had been out of touch for a long time with his nephew and could therefore give no news over him. The clergymen were surprised, since it was known what a close relationship the two usually had; the hope was therefore expressed that a small conflict is sometimes removed of itself. — The Dean replied, "there is no outlook of that, as it is not about misunderstandings or passing failures, but rather about life views which are against my principles, the teachings of Christianity and the laws of conventional honour." The clergymen regretted that and suggested though that all could turn out well again in that the views of men change so easily. — The Dean conceded that and said, "Provided he were alone, I would hope so; only he is in the claws of a tempter, a freemason, an atheist, who obstructs him from hearing the truth." — The clergymen, who could not comprehend how such an educated, good-natured man as the Assessor could be dominated by such a tempter, wanted to at least know the name of the latter in order to be able work against him in suitable cases. — The Dean responded, "It is a man who is called Doctor without though practising as a doctor and is called Wehrmann." — "Wehrmann?", the clergymen asked in astonishment. — "Yes," the Dean answered, "whom I do not wish to set eyes on." — The clergymen, who had distinctly heard the name Wehrmann with the introductions, directed embarrassed looks at the Doctor, as if it were asking him whether perhaps a mix-up of names had taken place, or whether there were not two Wehrmanns. — The Doctor did not change his demeanour, and if the embarrassment of the Parson Punter had made it impossible, he would probably have remained incognito and answered the Dean therein, thus he spoke, however, his eyes fixed on his opponent.

Doctor: "You seem not to know the Doctor in person?"
Dean: "No."
Doctor: "Then your judgement sounds hard from the mouth of a Christian, highly placed clergyman."
Dean: "What! You want to defend a Bible twister, a false teacher?"

Doctor: "I will be permitted to defend myself though?"
Dean: "What? You would be —"
Doctor: "The Doctor Wehrmann accused so severely by you."
Dean: "And you hold no inhibitions of pushing into the company of eight canonical priests?"
Doctor: "The priests, even if yet so canonical, are men, are my peers, and therefore I do not see why I should avoid them."
Dean: "The priests are servants of God and have no community with free-thinkers."
Doctor: "Have the priests a prerogative before God? — Are they expressly called by him as his servants, or have they received their credentials from men?"
Dean: "I don't know how you can begin to put such questions!" —
Doctor: "If my questions do not become you, then ask and I will answer."
Dean: "You are a Christian?"
Doctor: "Yes."
Dean: "You are a freemason?"
Doctor: "Yes."
Dean: "And yet you want to be a Christian! — Here you have been blinded by the lying devil."
Doctor: "How so?" —
Dean: "Because you have told me something which can never exist."
Doctor: "Why not?"
Dean: "Christianity is a church of God, freemasonry a hiding place of Satan."
Doctor: "You therefore know about freemasonry?"
Dean: "God preserve me from it."
Doctor: "And nevertheless you speak judgement over it?"
Dean: "Here it is easy to judge because you see its fruits."
Doctor: "Which fruits?"
Here the Dean became embarrassed. This stimulated him still more to vehemency and he answered, "Such fruits as you are."

Doctor: "Dear Dean, you allow yourself a language which I will not respond to as it deserves, out of reverence for the guests."

Dean: "I acknowledge here no right to hospitality. — This house is the property of the state, the residents of it belong to my diocese and hence I use the right of the householder and advise you to depart from our circle."

At these words Parson Punter stood up from his seat and said, "Dear Dean, you go too far!" — The other table guests seemed indeed to disapprove of the Dean's behaviour, but did not have the courage to express themselves out loud. — But the Doctor said, "Dear Dean, you have by means of your office declared this house outside the laws of hospitality and thereby given me full power not only to defend myself, but even to stride into the attack. So listen! — You call me an atheist! — There you lie! For I believe in God far more sincerely than you because I honour him also in the human, his image, whilst you, blinded by prejudice, express a sentence of damnation over the members of a society which you do not know at all. — You say I am a tempter! — If I were to want to prosecute you before the courts over this accusation, I would like to know with what you can justify such injuries. Finally you damn me as a freemason and do not consider that members of the consistory, some of the highest state officials, that even princes of our ruling house are as well. Do you also want to toss your excommunications at these people?"

The Dean responded fiercely, "I am not tossing. But God will toss them and his fury will not tire until they are exterminated from the earth."

With these words the Doctor rose from his seat and said, turning to the company, "My gentlemen! Forgive me if I now feel myself forced to leave you. My duty as a subject does not permit me to remain in company where it is spoken with such impropriety of the uppermost state officials and even of our august ruling house. — Heaven give you the courage to not grow cold under the crook of such a shepherd of souls in your sacred profession."

He took his hat and stick and left. — Parson Punter accompanied him to the door and expressed his regrets over the incident, and asked him to not make him pay for it. The Doctor called on him to be calm and to consider that a small lesson could not have harmed the Dean. He promised to come again as soon as he believed it had cooled off a little in the head of the latter. — He went outside, but the Parson returned with a morose look to the company. — A deep silence reigned as he entered. — Finally the Dean turned to him and said, "You have prepared an unpleasant day for me in that you drew a man, like the Doctor, into our company. I do not know how I am to interpret knowing you are in such company. I will have trouble removing again the adverse impression which I have felt." — The Parson replied, "Nobody has more to regret from this scene than I have, to the extent it occurred in my home where I had intended to honour my superior and rejoice with some of my worthy colleagues. For that reason will the good Dean allow me to absolve myself from what I am not guilty of and is a mere play of fate. — The Doctor, whom I have known a long time, came to visit me today for the first time, suspecting nothing so much as than meeting the good Dean. You came, recognised him from a side which does not seem to speak to his advantage, and thus we had to lament that two men who, on what basis I do not know, are enemies met today unexpectedly at my table."

The Dean, who caught the first moment to interrupt the Parson, now asked, "In what relationship do you stand to the Doctor?"

Parson: "In an amicable and very instructive one."

Dean: "What instruction could you receive from such a man?"

Parson: "That you would best learn from him himself, if you possess enough impartiality to speak with him."

Dean: "I do not want to speak to him and forbid you from contact with him."

Parson: "Dean!"

Dean: "It is to be stuck to and for every clergyman in my deanship."

Parson: "Without knowledge of the consistory?"

Dean: "I will make my report tomorrow."

Parson: "Dean, I allow myself to remark that I got to know the Doctor in the house of the member of the consistory

Wekham who treated him with honour and expressed to me especially that I should make use of the acquaintance made."

Dean: "What others do is no rule for me. I stand by my remarks." — The other clergymen, who also felt hit by such a ban, protested against it and declared that only the highest state authority could proscribe whose contact one had to avoid. — He saw himself pushed into a corner by this reply and said, "It is best I distance myself from company which seems to have united against me." He stood up and began to leave. — Parson Punter asked him to be calm and not to leave the parsonage which should be a house of peace. — "Among Belial's children no peace is possible," the Dean responded, and insisted on leaving. While yet for and against was being spoken and he was already at the door, the Doctor entered. The Deacon shrunk back, as much as he could, and cried out, "Do you seek to bring us still more into conflict?"

"I do not seek any conflict," the Doctor responded, "to the contrary, I wish to put you in a mood which befits a clergyman, a shepherd of peace, out of which I have brought you without intending to."

Dean: "You know long since that I know you, and you should not have stepped into my path."

Doctor: "I did not step into your path, you did into mine. Once already you have sought to bring suspicion on my convictions with one of your relations, without that I made a complaint over it. Today you insulted me personally in front of an honourable company without my giving you the slightest cause. This too I want to forget, provided you accept a suggestion which I will herewith make to you. Your zeal against me arises out of the errant opinion I am no Christian, am even a sort of antichrist. We will come to an understanding over this point and indeed in purely Christian ways. Give me an exercise from the gospels for written treatment; I will give you also one to the same end; impartial judges shall judge our works, and if it is found that I am on the wrong path, then I will turn around; but should you in your zeal have gone too far, you may wander your road, but leave me and all who join with me in peace."

Dean: "I should enter into a theological contest with a layman?"

Doctor: "Whoever avoids the contest is afraid of it."

Dean: "I am not afraid; nevertheless I will not accept your suggestion."

Doctor: "Then you should not have challenged me."

Dean: "To express one's convictions is no challenge."

Doctor: "Oh yes, if these convictions bring harm to another and injure his honour."

Dean: "I will not be led astray by niceties and reject your suggestion."

Doctor: "Then you must put up with me stepping out publicly as challenger and obtaining satisfaction for my honour."

Dean: "That you will not dare."

Doctor: "Oh yes, I will dare, and indeed with the knowledge and will of the consistory which has the duty to protect me from attacks on my honour from the side of their own. You have to choose: either among friends, or publicly."

The Dean wanted to answer with vehemence. But the clergymen sought to placate him, and moved him to accept the suggestion. He refused for a long time and uttered the most fierce threats. But since the Doctor stood by his declaration of making the matter public, and the clergymen considered it their duty, on account of the honour of their profession, to prevent such a thing, the pride of the Dean awoke and he said, "In order to show you, my good Doctor, that I do not fear your Bible wisdom, I give in to the wishes of my colleagues and accept your hubristic suggestion. Give me your exercise, then I will do the same, but under the condition that each of us works out both exercises so that the views may be appropriately compared and the mistakes discovered."

The Doctor responded, "I am satisfied with that. — The exercise which I wish to be worked on by you, Dean, consists of the first verse of the Gospel of John:

> In the beginning was the Word, and the Word was with God, and the Word was God."

The Dean suggested indeed that this exercise had already been worked over in so many ways and from so many sides that nothing new was to be said over it anymore. But he agreed to the work and said, "The exercise I set consists of the words:

Not every one that saith unto me, Lord, Lord, shall enter into the kingdom of heaven; but he that doeth the will of my Father which is in heaven.*"

The Doctor wrote down the words and said, "Thank you, Dean, for the choice of exercise. It is only to be asked now, who shall be the judges?" — The Dean replied, "About that, in order to relieve me of all advantage, here my good colleagues may decide." — The Doctor said, "I am satisfied with that. — But now away with all the rancour. Before the manner of a duel between two parties is decided, they say to one another still acrimonious things; but as soon as everything is in order, they eat and drink with one another and are as happy as if they were the best of friends. — So too will we act. I have done you out of an amusing day; I wish to make this good again, even if only for a cheerful hour."

The Dean did not respond to this. But finally the Doctor succeeded in producing a bearable mood through his demeanour which was able to seep into all situations. — They remained another two hours and then parted like two fighters who were having a good feast before the fight. — The Doctor stayed overnight with Parson Punter and told him in advance the meaning of the two set exercises. The latter felt very obliged for that, but feared that the offered interpretation would distance the Dean still more and reinforce his prejudices. The Doctor, however, was of a different opinion and did not give up hope of illuminating the orthodox mind of his opponent a little.

***

---

* [Tr.: Matthew 7:21.]

The Self Perspective

When the three friends had assembled one evening again at the Doctor's, he made them aware of the adventure he had had and the contest he had taken on. They rejoiced over it, only they doubted whether the suggested judges would possess enough freedom of spirit to enter into the ideas of the Doctor. The Professor suggested that if the matter did not turn out entirely to his advantage, there was still the opportunity to say much which would otherwise remain hidden. He expressed further that he rejoiced over this contest because it could be nothing but beneficial to loosen the blindfolds a little of such orthodox clergymen who were constantly more of a hindrance to a good cause than unbelief and rationalism. — The Assessor and the Deacon were indeed not neutral over this prospective victory of the Doctor, only something else now lay on their hearts over which they would like an explanation. — Namely a few days before "Zschokke's Images of the Inner Gaze"* had appeared in the bookstores, which by necessity had to excite a great furore because it came from a man known to Germany as a scholar and poet, to his fatherland as a sterling patriot, and to all friends of truth as an effective fighter against obscurity. — They presented the matter to the Doctor with all the accompanying circumstances, along with the comment that after such phenomena a new realm must open up for prophecy because the facts were not allowed to be drawn into doubt.

The Doctor, who had not yet set eyes on the book, but who had already heard much of the aforementioned mental capabilities of Zschokke, let himself be told a few details of the contents and asked whether perhaps a guide to obtaining this state was contained in the book. — When they had answered in the negative to this, he began, "Zschokke belongs amongst the geniuses of our time; but as the distinguished naturally

---

* [Tr.: naturalised Swiss reformer and writer Johann Heinrich Daniel Zschokke (1771–1848). His autobiographical work *Eine Selbstschau* [A Self Reflection] (1842) may be being referenced here.]

gifted seldom worry about theory, so to does Zschokke carry on and practises the most sublime art of humanity as a mere dilettante. It is indeed indubitable that everything lies in the human, and everybody can draw everything from themselves; only some reveal with their inquiries certain advantages which lead us closer to the nature of the spirit and preserve us from error. — To record these advantages, to specify the shortest paths is then the task of those geniuses in order to establish thereby specific rules, that is, a theory, by which fellow men and posterity can instruct themselves. It is a pity that Zschokke, who would be the man for it, has not done such a thing; and if some reproach can be made of him, then it is on account of this neglect. But we owe him too much thanks to not have to silence every censure because he had the courage to reveal the workings of his talent in a time when every freedom of spirit is spoken of with mockery, where you only see freedom in the denial of spiritual characteristics and strive to reach the goal of life in the care of social and material goals. — Zschokke has given us a testimony which for our times has more worth than all the books of the world, because we see through his personality as it were with our own eyes and feel urged to seek his genius in ourselves and to form a theory from many different experiences.

Everything which the human does in life rests on the powers of nature. These powers are recognised, placed on firm principles which show us the elements of an art or science and lead us stepwise to mastery. Wisdom, freedom of spirit, spiritual activity of inward seeing, hearing and feeling, being born again, and prophecy are indeed different names, but are only *one* power in which the art of living and the basis of all positive knowledge is contained.

To the extent that we want to proceed thoroughly, we must say repeatedly that the human possesses by means of language cognitive ability, because if he could not speak, he would have to forget and subsequently lose all the impressions he receives from without and within. The root of all cognition seems according to this to lie in the language tools in that we could not speak without them. — Now, however, it is to be asked, who built these organs? Did they arise by accident and become used by humanity? — That would be directly as if we wanted to say the musical organ arose accidentally and the organ player used the accident and learnt to play the organ. — The music lies in the inner being of the human. — This music has made a point since time immemorial of constantly helping to produce new instruments in order to reveal itself. — In such a way did the organ arise. Lips, tongues, and throat are the tools of speaking; an inner, creative language has built these tools and uses them with the same freedom as the organist uses the keyboard of the organ.

Here one indeed says: spiritual powers and musical talent are not to be compared with one another. Anyone who says that is an orthodox mystic because he separates the powers of human nature from each other and each directs a single facet of activity. — The powers of the human are not to be separated in that even one and the same power can work spiritually and creaturely. — The hearing reflector for the notes and chords of music is in the inner being of the human, and it lifts the musician to the production of art. — The ABC of language is in the inner being of the human, and by means of it we can think and speak and even receive inner truths. — The light which is the actual bearer of notes and words reflects itself in its colours and forms no less than notes and words in the inner being of the human, from which then those miracle-like phenomena arise which we see in the Bible and in the experiences of Zschokke."

Those present expressed their satisfaction with this explanation; only they suggested that if it were so natural, more examples should be found amongst humanity. The Doctor responded, "It is by the half-heartedness with which one treats spiritual subjects in the learning institutions surprising that we see even single rays of the original light. For what does he who ascribes a positive action, an open seeing, hearing and feeling, have to expect? — Mockery and the accusation: sinister man and mystic! — But anyone who claims that God has been able to create without sight an eye, without hearing an ear, and without feeling feelings; anyone who furthermore claims that you can produce with seasonal seeds eternal fruits, with absurd, irrational seeds highest reason, they render homage to the teachings of the day and are revered as free-thinkers, if not even as a philosopher. — The spirit sees, hears, and feels; the body receives it from it. The spirit forms, speaks, and touches us, and through that alone we are capable of recognising it. Anyone who wants to conclude otherwise would make the sun the spreader of darkness, but the darkness into an illuminating sun. — Away with such irrational views which can entirely capture humans in an incomprehensible way. Nature is before our eyes! The spirit is in it, for nature is formed by it just as nature is in it in that nature serves it as nourishment from which it draws ever new sparks of wisdom and life."

Here the Doctor ended. — The Deacon wanted to present a few notes about his elemental exercises, but they found no favour. Thus they parted when the Doctor gave the promise of sharing the news as soon as the contest with the Dean had completely opened. The friends thanked him for this assurance and left.

***

The Contest

When the aforesaid friends had assembled again at the Doctor's, the contest had already begun and the latter was asked to reveal the interim result of it. He did not wait to be asked and began.

"The good Dean's hands were shaking, and he seemed not to have had any rest anymore until he had put his gospel knowledge to rest. On this basis the suggested contest judges, the clergymen, were not an adequate guarantee for him, and he transferred the entire matter to the consistory. From what viewpoint the latter consider the affair, I do not know yet. Meanwhile he worked up the promised essays and sent them to the Parson Punter who discussed it and my views with the other clergymen, but wanted to abstain from any judgement for as long as until they were clear over the attitude of the consistory. I have the essays of the Dean to hand and will share with you, provide it interests you, the main points of their content." — The friends requested it, and after he had fetched the papers from his desk, he began:

"You recall still the exercises which the Dean and I set one another at our peculiar meeting. The theme given by me was explained by him in the following way at the start of his work:

> In the beginning was the Word, and the Word was with God, and the Word was God. — It follows from this that Christ was already in the beginning, because Christ alone is the word. The word is the son of the father and God like him. Since now Christ is the word, he must also be God like the father. He is also God, for through him, through the word, the entire world is created. For this reason Christ came, when he came into the world, into his possession. Were he not the creator of the world, then it could not be his possession. In this way the original presence of God in the person of Christ is resolved in the most complete way, and we must not doubt anymore in his divinity.

And the Word was with God. — Here the presence of God seems to separate into two presences: into the word and into God. Only with exact consideration you find that word and God are just one thing, in that to be God without word and the word without God, no world could have been created. Both are contained within one another so intimately that they comprise one presence. — And in that lies the eternal love of the father for the human race, that he sent his son, that is, a part of himself, in order to save the sinning humans. We will work out in further detail this high, divine mission in the following and support it with the most conclusive evidence of gospel texts.

And the Word was God. — In this sentence it expresses what Christ is. He is the word, and since God is the word, he is God. — According to the meaning of the words the father seems to be contained himself in the son, in Christ. He is also contained in him; for Christ says himself: I am in the Father, and the Father in me*. — The entire difference between father and son consists in that the latter has become flesh in order to take the sins of the world on himself. This too will be explained still more clearly in the course of this discussion. —

This is the word for word start to the treatment of the first verse of the gospel of John. In the following it is extensively worked out and supported with citations in which you see the skilful theologian. The idea of the word leads him to the emergence of creation from chaos, in which Christ as son of the father was already active. The father namely saw in the beginning that the archangel Lucifer will fall, and in the place where he previously reigned, a new race, humanity, will arise and, seduced by the breath of the left behind atmosphere, will surrender itself to sins which can then not be wiped out except by becoming human, by crucifixion and death of the eternal son, the word.

In this same way he also treats his own chosen theme: Not every one that saith unto me, Lord, Lord, shall enter into the

---

*   [Tr.: John 14:11.]

kingdom of heaven; but he that doeth the will of my Father which is in heaven.

The will of the father, the explanation of which he seems to have directed the closest attention to, he describes, amongst much else, word for word in the following way:

> The will of the father, however, is to believe in his son, in Christ; believe that this one is of eternity and will be in eternity; that he climbed from heaven as perfect God, became man, wandered among men under the name 'Jesus of Nazareth', nourished himself with earthly food, died for the sins of humanity on the cross, arose from the dead, and went to heaven, but during his earthly career was God and God remained in perfect power, wisdom, and love and served humanity thereby as an exemplar for a divine transformation. Furthermore the will of the father is that we all believe unconditionally what Christ and his apostles, illuminated by the Holy Spirit, spoke, without presuming to judge and presuming neither to take the least from it, nor to do anything with it. Those are just the sins from which humanity must be saved so that they make no foreign gods, keep their vain reason in check, and child-like, trusting in the Saviour's death, abandon themselves full of humility to the guidance of the one crucified. —

The Dean expresses himself in this sense over the being of Christ with the consequence, which is only to be regretted, that he does not know the foundation which was laid for the Christian church, and hence must by necessity build in the wrong direction. Where he speaks of Christian love, you are almost tempted to consider him to be a shepherd of souls who is filled with spirit; but when he comes to the chapter on damnation he becomes a firestorm which is threatening to consume everybody who does not believe his words."

The lecture on these two essays had of course had the effect on the audience which must by necessity follow when you see yourself whilst on the path to religious freedom being threatened at once with being bound in iron shackles. — They expressed their views openly about it and could not comprehend how they could have lived previously in similar darkness, since the inadmissibility of such a system must also be illuminating to the less practised mind. They asked the Doctor to also read them his two essays. He responded, "What I express here in writing, I have already said to you enough times. It is about the basic principle of the entire doctrine, about the word. To anyone who does not know this, my essay is a hieroglyph; but to someone who knows it, it must be like the carpenter who understands how to erect a house. — My essay begins in the following way:

In the beginning was the Word. — Where is the beginning? With every act of creation. — What is the word? This is the act of creation which flies around in the chaos in lines and colours, mixed with lightning, and thereby expresses itself. It is the eternal elemental power which creates and forms everything and raises the human to thinking. — It is the eternal prophet who resides in us and unveils to us the secrets of creation and the teachings of Christ. It is that possession of the human which he must preserve should his freedom and his independence remain to him. This word was the beginning.

And the Word was with God. — Here the hieroglyph becomes darker because we see God separated into two parts: into God and word. Only it clears itself up soon when we consider the word as an attribute of God and God as the possessor of it. God is the confluence or the sun of the language elements, but the word is the use of them in his innumerable compositions. In this way word and God are only one thing, and we are forced to add the third phrase:

And the Word was God.

Thus sounded the beginning of my first essay. The following does not carry so clearly anymore the stamp of my views, because, in order to be comprehensible to the contest judges, I had to hold myself more to the school, and hence I deem it superfluous to spoil the time with reading it aloud. We will rather remain a few more moments with what was said before in order to discuss the sense of it as much as possible.

The Contest

In the beginning was the Word, and the Word was with God, and the Word was God. — According to the clear sense of these words, those who know the word must also know God, because the closing part expressly says: and the Word was God. Now the question just arises whether that which formerly was will also still be in our time? The question is easily and satisfactorily answered to the extent the talk is about God, and God was of eternity and will be in eternity. Hence, if God was the word, then he is it still. Another question arises accordingly, and that is: how does one hear the word? — Here you must refer the questioner to the Bible, where he finds such in all circumstances, in large as in small, in the individual and in the general. — But why do we not now hear this word anymore? — Here you must answer with the words of the prophet Amos, whose prophecy has arrived unfortunately in the highest degree. He says in Amos 8:11–12:

> Behold, the days come, saith the Lord God, that I will send a famine in the land, not a famine of bread, nor a thirst for water, but of hearing the words of the Lord:
> And they shall wander from sea to sea, and from the north even to the east, they shall run to and fro to seek the word of the Lord, and shall not find it.

We do not hear the word anymore because orthodoxy twists it and has overfilled our soul in such a way with dogmatic sanctuaries that we are frightened of free, natural truth and do not have the courage anymore to gaze at its original brilliance. We do not hear it anymore because reason, too busy with sensual impressions and ideas, cannot bear its pure light anymore and withdraws from it with all the cleverness which stands at its command.

Shall this state persist for a long time yet? — Shall then, in a time when all branches of science and ability stand in the most magnificent full bloom, this divine branch, this crown of all knowledge, the eternal word, not also be again drawn into the light of day and worked on? — We call ourselves Christians — Christianity is a school of prophets. — We call ourselves Christians — Christianity is the doctrine of the word, but not only the written, but also that given by the spirit which Christ called the "holy". Do we want to go longer without the necessary predicate of a Christian and be content with the empty name? — No, we want, even if only in small number, to realise the highest which humanity can have in ourselves again so that those who circulate from one sea to the next can console themselves and say: the dismal time of prophecy is over and the lost word is found again."

The Doctor concluded his lecture here. None of those present made any reply to it. The Doctor, who was struck by this silence, said, "You must excuse me if, instead of teaching, I sometimes lapse into declamations. — But, who in a city where he sees famished residents can remain calm of heart and curb his speech?"

The freed friends shared this view and vowed, at least for themselves, to make an end to this dismal state. The Deacon uttered especially, "Good Doctor! Reassure yourself; I am so surely on the trail of the matter that I hope to be able to show you results soon." — The others promised not to fall behind the Deacon and to ask him to be their guide with entering on the correct path.

The Doctor found this unity very expedient and said, "Travel together, then the path becomes all the easier for you."

They parted, and the three friends discussed along the way the manner of getting in touch with the Deacon in order to get to know his Pestalozzian process."

***

The Correspondence

The Doctor had gone for a few months into the countryside because he felt freer there and could fulfil his spiritual activity unhindered there. — He had instructed the Professor to deal with everything which could happen with respect to the Dean or to report to him. Thus several months passed without anything considerable happening or being spoken of. The three friends had indeed often come together, but their discussions turned about what they had heard from the Doctor and so they made no use of it than at most sharpening their memory. In this quandary they arranged to start a correspondence with the Doctor, partly in order to learn something new and partly also in order to have the views of the Doctor in writing before their eyes. The Deacon undertook to lead the correspondence, and had already had the following letter sent to the Doctor the next day.

Deacon to the Doctor

Dear Sir etc.

We feel since your departure like a small flock without shepherds. We have indeed already discussed several times the matter which is the most important to us, only we lack that spiritual authority which draws the words from the realm of the spirit and sets aside every opposition in advance. Hence we have decided to ask you that we may write to you and expect from you, even if only a single time, answer and instruction. I begin therefore with stating to you my previously won views in respect to an elemental doctrine of our matter, in order to put you in a position to separate the right from the erroneous and to provide me with your paternal reprimands. I promise in advance that everything you say to me will also be said to my friends in that we have given each other our word to hold firmly to one another on our pilgrimage to the temple of truth.

You, my highly esteemed patron, were the one who brought my attention to the possibility of an elemental method by means of which one would be capable of recognising the spirit of the Christian religion. This idea straightaway took up all my attention. I dedicated to its investigation several hours a day and often entire nights. — What are the elements of the Christian religion, I asked myself constantly, and believed at first to have found them in the three pillars of its church: faith, hope, and love. But how are these characteristics to be obtained, tended and exercised in proper measure was my second question. I tormented myself, only the faith did not become stronger, the hope not more consoling, and the love not warmer. I inquired after basic concepts of theology and philosophy at the same time and found that with the dissection of every concept a crowd of things are discovered over which we are unable to provide any information. I said to myself: crooked and straight lines and angles are the elements of geometry and the notes of the scales of music; where do I find something of that sort in the realm of thought, of faith, in one word, in the realm of religion? — I now sought in the names of the saints, the apostles, in the name of Christ and even the prophets an elemental power which is capable of pointing me to the beginning of the matter. — I must confess, in this activity I obtained something which I did not know how to interpret at the time and only recently obtained clarity over. It was strange how all these names which I especially selected from the Bible expressed themselves in the mouth, penetrated down through the throat into the belly, from there drawing in all directions through the body and exciting in me sometimes pleasant, but sometimes also painful sensations. I did not know how to interpret such phenomena at the time, but now I feel that that must have been a useful preparatory work for me in that from that moment when you brought my attention to the emperor Y-a-o, that is to the letters, I found and thus recognised infallibly the elemental thing, just as I know that I must move my feet to walk.

I present to you these observations of mine, not in the intention of asking you whether they are right, for here no mistake is possible anymore; but to ask you to give me a few hints on how to treat the elements still more fundamentally, to set them in a sort of scales on which one can stride with surer step to open knowledge, to mastery.

The friends to whom I have read aloud this letter, which they are not yet capable of digesting though, give their regards to you with complete devotion; I, however, remain etc.

The Doctor to the Deacon

Your letter has given me heartfelt joy in that I could see from it that you are not only on the trail of truth, but already in its temple. Only you are lacking still the special view of all parts of the temple which is necessary to draw proper use of it. For this elucidation a few words will suffice; therefore pay attention.

I have at our meetings often said language is the highest gift of humanity. To get to know this not only in the spoken, but also in the organic elements is an essential condition for a true servant of the church.

The organic elements of language are lips, teeth, tongue, and throat. These are, like the letters themselves, so firmly grounded in nature that none can take the place of the others. With the lips you cannot say D, with the tongue not B, with the throat neither. Just as little, however, are you in a position to express a K or Ch* with the lips, teeth, or tongue. — Pay attention here! It is of the greatest importance in that we are thereby put in a position to penetrate into the inner being of nature and to investigate its spiritual powers.

The lips are representatives of the skin and muscles of the human. The teeth form the feeding branch of the bone system. The tongue stands in the closest connection with the inner organs of the body, with the veins, the blood, even with the nerves. The throat finds itself constantly in a rearmost corner or in the centre of a matter.

All that is bears the stamp of these four organic elements. Each thing has an outer, an appending, an inner, and a medial element. — We feel the upper layer of the earth, when we bring it into our mind, as lips; the old mountains with their peaks and rock which passes through the entire earth as teeth and bones; behind these rocky scrags we feel the tongue, and

---

* [Tr.: the German *ch* sound referred to here is similar to that in the Scottish word lo*ch*.]

the centre of the earth we can imagine distinctly only by means of the throat.

Take these few things. To an elemental man, like yourself, the use will be easy. — But share the content of this letter only slowly with your friends so that they are not scared off by the simplicity and the unusualness of it. I give my regards to you and the friends with sincere friendship and esteem etc.

Deacon to the Doctor

I have shared with our friends the conclusion of your richly substantive letter in which the greeting, but also at the same time the warning to go slowly with the work is contained. They responded to the greeting with sincere reverence, over the slow striding forward they are not indignant because the content of my letter to you still occupies them too much. In particular it is not clear to the Professor that it is possible to awaken spiritual powers with technical means. I have already often remarked the more rationality, the greater the orthodoxy, or vice versa where one becomes super rational from utter orthodoxy. But he must get to work, and he wants to, only he asks to have patience with him when his wanting to be all too clever leads him out of bounds. — The Assessor progresses quickly, and if it will ever be possible for him to put into words his idealised ideal then we will have obtained everything.

I have investigated practically your magnificent, unalterable system fixed in nature, with lips, teeth, tongue, and throat and found it so completely proven that I do not comprehend why one does not have it in every school to thereby prepare the children for an inner, religious life which alone will lead humanity to immortality.

Concerning my other activity, I can say that I sometimes hear the word clearly within me. But it does not always tell the truth; what is to be done there?

Of the Dean, we hear only so much that the consistory shelved its entry and gave him an admonition not to injure the general tolerance.

Do not forget us and take the views etc.

The Doctor to the Deacon

I have a small incident to report to you which can be of good effect for our good Professor.

You know the village M...t, the lovely valley in which it lies, the clear stream which flows past it, the beautiful heights all around from which you see over the area like in a magic mirror. Drawn by these beauties you see around this time of year always a few townsfolk there who use the healthy air and pleasant area as a sort of cure in order to strengthen themselves for the winter stay in the city. Among these was found a man who in a sort of philosophical pride worried little about the others and sometimes made short excursions on foot for himself sometimes here, sometimes there. For me it was also directly not to do with large groups, and I acted just like the aforementioned man. We met a few times on our wanderings, finally decided to begrudge each other a word and to ask, 'You are also making use of the beautiful day again today? — It seems this path is the most pleasant to you?' and so on. After a few such conversations, we once walked next to each other for quarter of an hour without exactly leading any special discourse. The man became of interest for me and, as it seemed, I no less for him. When we met each other again and the first greetings given before were over, I asked him, "You do not seem to be at home here?"

Him: "No."

Me: "What business draws you into this area?"

Him: "None."

Me: "When one has no special business, one often works the most."

Him: "I have worked a lot and am presently before my goal."

Me: "Resting perhaps on your laurels?"

Him: "No, in no respect. I stand in a conflict with the world where you must not expect any laurels."

Me: "Forgive me, it was not my intention to delve into secrets."

Him: "I have no secrets; to the contrary, I am uncovering to many secrets."

I now fell silent in that I considered him to be a politician whom one seemed not right to approach and therefore let him roam about so solitarily. My taciturnity attracted his attention, and hence he said, "Don't misjudge me when I tell you that I stand in a conflict with humanity. This is of a sort that, since we no longer have any spiritual inquisition, the entire world may know it. I stand namely in a dispute with the clergy because I claimed their activities were of no use, and it would be just as good if they weren't there at all."

Now it was clear to me what sort of man I had before me. That is a rationalist of our time, I thought, and got busy with seeing how far infected he already was. I therefore said, "There you might not be wrong."

Him: "Unfortunately I am right; but I know no means of influencing the evil."

Me: "Every positive evil consumes itself."

Him: "And because the clergy does not wipe itself out, do you consider it to be a positive evil?"

Me: "I am of such a peculiar nature that it would be difficult for me to believe in a positive evil."

Him: "Then you are a philanthropist of that good-natured sort who always hopes and even when they see themselves betrayed every day."

Me: "This sort of philanthropy seems to be a natural disposition."

Him: "No, good sir, that it is not, otherwise I would have to still possess it. I loved all humanity, without exception. I saw the image of God in it and would have been in a position to sacrifice myself for it; but unfortunately I was awoken from my beautiful dream and see nothing about myself but the deceived and deceivers."

Me: "Then you must unmask the deceivers."

Him: "That would surely be my goal if it were able to be achieved. But to get mixed up in a struggle with the deceivers means nothing less than storming Olympus and plunging Jupiter's throne into the abyss."

Me: "Jupiter has already fallen."

Him: "He, no! He reigns still in his stolen majesty, but under a different name, unchallenged and sovereign as ever."

Me: "You mean the majesty of the offered faith sits on Jupiter's throne?"

The Correspondence

Him: "So it does. You have understood me and will agree with me."

Me: "Your claim has admittedly some truth; but I cannot agree with you entirely unconditionally."

Him: "Not? — Then I will remain silent in that I do not want to put you into that desolation where indeed the sun alone illuminates the truth, but whose rays, instead of warming, dry out the heart."

I made no reply to this phrase; for now I knew my man and had merely to think of how he was to be gotten the better of and might have the crust blown away from his heart.

We spoke over other, insignificant topics. Finally he turned back to the village, but I climbed up another rise in order to see the fall of the sun in its fullest majesty.

The man seemed to avoid me for a few days, for he had chosen another side of the area for his walks. Finally he returned. — The heart, which can never entirely suppress the pigheaded rationality, seemed to have drawn him again into my path. He greeted me amicably, and after he had explained to me that the area on the other side of the heights did not look as beautiful, he came to the people, to speaking of them in their errors and weaknesses, and finally again speaking of spirituality. He indeed apologised when he touched this theme; I replied to him, however, that he need not feel embarrassed in that I possessed in this respect such a good stomach as to be able to bear even food appearing indigestible. He rejoiced over my tolerance, or, in that he corrected himself, my broad-mindedness in that he claimed the greatest misfortune of humanity consisted in not wanting to hear the truth.

I replied to this that I approved of his judgement, only I could not unite with everyone's views over the concept "truth" because some seek the truth in an impenetrable labyrinth filled to overflowing with objects, others though in a sandy desert. The man stopped short and asked me to which class I surely numbered him? — I answered, to the second. — At this answer, he looked me calmly in the face and said, "You are not entirely wrong; only it is not so desolate on my side as one thinks. The human is born, grows up amidst childish joys and tended by loving parents. Then he steps into life, rejoices over his effectiveness, rejoices over the good that he creates; fortune then gives him a decent wife and nice children, so it would be wrong to not be thankful for such a life course."

I looked my man calmly in the face as he spoke, in order to see whether his demeanour did not put the lie to the words. I did not notice the slightest. Finally I said, "Immortality is a high fortune, even if it is not realised and we only believe in it."

Him: "Blind faith is under all circumstances an evil."

Me: "I knew a young man who was the son of wealthy parents whose wealth, however, he lost through frequent cases of misfortune and was pushed into the deepest poverty. He had nothing in his misfortune but the certain outlook of the inheritance of a rich uncle. — This thought, I would like to say, this faith in a favourable turn to his fate gave him strength, even often joy, to bear all the afflictions of poverty and to preserve his soul's peace."

Him: "Now, and was his faith justified? Were his hopes fulfilled? — For to see oneself betrayed in such expectations must be the bitterest thing!"

Me: "He died before his uncle."

Him: "So vain are the phantoms of faith and hope."

Me: "But they give ease through the magic of a beautiful outlook." —

Him: "Probably to those who wander in error, in the darkness. I confess to you that I consider such a darkness to be more conducive than the sunlight in the middle of the day when you cannot seek enough shade. But someone who stands in such heat of the sun, should they thus despair?"

Me: "They should, as you yourself noted, build a beneficent hut or arbour in order to rest comfortably in the shade there."

Him: "How does one build such huts and arbours?"

Me: "With the faith in immortality."

Him: "On what does this faith base itself?"

Me: "On a positive freedom of spirit of humanity."

Him: "On freedom of spirit? — If that were so, reason, which actually makes up the spirit, would have to have provided information about it."

Me: "As soon as reason unites with the feelings of faith and of love, then the information will not be lacking."

Him: "Here humans build on sand, on a priestly doctrine which at all times deceives humanity in order to assuage their ambition, their thirst for power, their avarice, their lusts, in a word, all the urges to which the animal nature of humans can drive them."

Me: "The thought that there is a class of men who from their origin on are only intent on deceiving their fellow men and feasting at their cost strikes so much against my feeling that I cannot agree absolutely with you here."

Him: "Then show me a basis for the priestly dominance of all times and nations if it is not the cited one."

Me: "The basis of their dominance exists in the dignity of their calling."

Him: "Who has called them?"

Me: "Who has called them — in the correct answering of this question lies the solution of the puzzle. A few say God himself has called them; others say the spirit; a third party awards the honour to the mind and reason; a fourth builds on inner feelings in that they claim these are an admonition of God. There is yet another party who go to work quite simply and directly claim that the recognition of God, the nature of religion, and the high calling of the clergy rests on self-knowledge."

Him: "That must be a self-knowledge of a peculiar sort if it should be capable of explaining this."

Me: "It is not that self-knowledge where we just tell ourselves we are better and brighter than those others; or where you think to have risen in the pit of one's life, when you can tell yourself whether you are of calm or fierce temperament, whether you are industrious or idle, vengeful or good-natured, etc., but rather where we are able to recognise the receptivity of our nature to also receive spiritual impressions and, please note, to also feel them so exactly that we can make use of them in every moment."

Him: "How is that? — This expression is so new to me that I cannot even comprehend the literal sense. A receptivity of which we are conscious, the spiritual impressions which we feel and receive at the same time, and which we can make use of in every moment. Is it not so?"

Me: "Approximately. But in order to make the matter more comprehensible, we will, if you are not against it, investigate it practically."

The man became wide-eyed and measured me from head to toe as if he wanted to investigate whether I, like other people, stood on two legs, and asked in a tone of astonishment, "Investigate practically?"

Me: "Of course. What rational man would believe something which he had not tested?"

Him: "You speak in a more and more puzzling way. You want to make tests of a receptivity by means of which you feel spiritual impressions?"

Me: "That is what I said. It just comes down to you undertaking such a test."

Him: "What do I have to thereby do?"

Me: "Nothing but be extremely natural and only answer to the questions which I place with the greatest honesty."

Him: "You are becoming more and more incomprehensible. Are you perhaps a sorcerer?" —

Me: "I am no sorcerer, but rather a rationalist who, if one says to him, deep in the earth there are gold mines — there the gold arises through the union and fixing of the rays of the sun into a compact bright metal — does not oppose, but rather bores a shaft, climbs down, and convinces himself that the sun truly reflects itself under the earth and produces a simile of its purity."

Him: "That is a fitting image. Only, I long for the test."

Me: "You are thus seriously determined?"

Him: "Yes."

Me: "And will, without pondering beforehand, without considering beforehand, give answers to my questions according to your feeling?"

Him: "Yes."

Me: "I must make one more remark in advance. The matter which we are undertaking is so easy that a child passes it infallibly. For the aged pretend-philosopher tainted with prejudices it can miscarry."

Him: "I beg, get on with it."

Me: "Well now, then listen. — I ask, when you imagine the tip of our church tower, where do you feel it?"

Him: "In the head of course."

Me: "But when you imagine the deep foundations of the tower, where do you feel it then?"

Here the man questioned stopped short and answered, "Strange! In the feet."

Me: "When you admit the low-hanging branch of this tree into your imagination, where do you feel it?"

Him: "In the shoulders."

Me: "And the roots of the tree?"

Him: "Again in the feet."

Me: "Thank you. You have done your thing well."

He began spontaneously to laugh here and asked, "To where shall that lead?"

Me: "To convincing you that spiritual impressions are possible. Neither the foundation of the tower, nor the roots of the tree touched you, and nonetheless you have felt them."

Him: "And the use of that?"

Me: "We are taught and accustomed from youth on to seeking God in the heights, to imagining him in the heights; through that he climbs into the head where we think him through and process him for so long until he finally dissolves and vanishes for us. God is everywhere; the whole man, that is the entire form of the human, must learn to feel him, then we will also have him entirely. He must stir in the feet, knees, ankles, hips, thighs, in the belly, in the chest and the back, yes even in all the organs right down to the marrow in the bones, then we will feel him, feel our positive life, and immortality will become not only possible, but a necessity. The head is the tip of the tower, is the rooster on it which cries out into the world and directs itself according to every wind; which looks over everything, but is also seen everywhere. In the tower itself is the clock which goes according to firmly fixed rules and measures minutes, hours, and days. All this, however, could not be provided that it did not stand on a firm foundation, on steady feet. I ask you to consider this, to practise a little, and you will find the test confirmed."

Him: "I felt what you said, and nevertheless I must stick to my claim and say it is impossible. How is it conceivable that we should learn to recognise God or the spirit firstly in the feet?"

Me: "Whether it is conceivable for us or not, it is yet nothing but. — Though I ask further, entreat you, however, to set your face to the south. — When you imagine the rise of the sun, where do you feel it?"

Him: "On my left side."

Me: "And the setting of it?"

Him: "On the right."

Me: "I ask further, where do you feel the land of our antipodes?"

Him: "At the feet."

Me: "And where the sky over the antipodes?"

Him: "Also at the feet, but in a great arc."

Me: "What ideas will be purer now, those which we draw directly from the clouds above us or those which we draw from under us, through the entire earth to us?"

Him: "The latter."

Me: "Can you imagine something still purer that that is?"

Him: "No."

Me: "The purest of all which the human can imagine and at the same time feel is the spirit of God. To awaken and refine the receptivity of feeling naturally is self-knowledge, but what is felt is God whose recognition all founders of religions and spiritual institutions had as their goal."

Him: "And this would be the basis on which the religions and their priesthoods rested?"

Me: "It is."

Him: "Why do we see no trace of such a doctrine?"

Me: "Because it has been lost, and we hope to obtain everything with the rooster on the tower."

Him: "I know enough and will examine it."

With these words the conversation was broken off. I consider myself convinced in having given the arch-rationalist the full charge, and began to talk about the beautiful weather. He said good evening to me after a few responses and returned to the village.

Read this aloud to your friends and tell the good Professor before the reading, I ask him to listen very attentively and to examine the contained lessons through self-enacted tests.

I give my regards to you all and I assure you of my esteem and friendship.

Deacon to the Doctor

I believe such a sensation as your letter brought forth, not only in the Professor, but in all of us, could simply not have been brought forth by another letter, as much as has already been written in the world even. — The Professor could barely recover from his astonishment. — The Assessor said that we seek for our inquiries and ways of working an ideal, meanwhile we have one before us in our esteemed friend and patron, the good Doctor, who could not be more perfect. — But I said that now I comprehend at once why the ancients never placed their divine services at the midday hour, but instead always in the morning or the evening. — The Mithraists and Pythagoreans greeted the sun at its rising and let this sublime phenomenon work on their bodies, meanwhile the horizon also brightened over their heads. The first Christians chose the night, and the Catholics still celebrate the birth of Christ at midnight. If we imagine the high midday of the antipodes to be the time of our midnight, then we feel enclosed all around in a vault of light which cannot but work beneficially, nourishingly, invigoratingly, and instructively on us.

Our meetings are regularly once a week, and we become bit by bit so comfortable that we sometimes forget that our high-minded friend and teacher is not among us. — It is remarkable how the language gradually develops with us. Over topics on which we have not previously thought, we hold lectures over which a professor of rhetoric could rejoice. Is that a consequence of the exercise or of the word stirring in us? — It must be the last, for in other company we feel, at least I do, still as awkward and dumb as before; but as soon as I begin to speak about our matter with erect body, sometimes with the hand placed on the belly or the chest, then it is just as if the words were flowing out of a spring. The Professor has noticed something similar with himself too and already declared that it is often just as if an orator were in him whom he was just repeating after. With the Assessor it progresses slower because the ideal which he has fabricated still stands too high above all these phenomena. Only we know, taught by such successes, now clearly what it means to free the genius of your own knowledge in yourself and to take it as a teacher. Often we learn amongst ourselves in that we make deductions to which one could not have arrived with every cleverness and every meditation. It is truly a power of thought, a genius, a living word in humans which wants only to be free in order to give us information on everything which concerns God and immortality. — I have often asked in our gatherings whether such experiences are not worth more than all book learning.

Over the cause of why the word in me does not always speak the truth to my questions, I have provided myself with information in that I penetrated into myself for as long as until it became clear to me. — At a place where there are more echoes, the best music does not give any pure notes, nor intelligible melodies and nor proper chords. — The word must surely penetrate as if through echoes of many kinds until it reaches us? Hence we must smooth the walls, remove the outgrowths, fill in the shallows, so that the sound of the word can be heard without disturbance and interruption. I have also obtained the conviction that we must not become doubtful about this unreliability of the word at first, as the art of being able to speak has greater worth than that which one speaks. And does not the child speak, does not everybody speak who learns a language, in the first stages also wrongly? — Nature, you have often told us, is our teacher, and precisely through that we rediscover in the realm of the spirit the same norm according to which visible nature works, the confluence of God and the creation is preserved whereby we obtain for our actions a visible test.

Forgive me that I write so teacher-like, as if I were to have much that was new to tell you. But it is too comfortable to feel free to be able to speak as one feels, and to see oneself freed from the dust of school. Only now do I understand fully the verse with which Homer opens the talk of his heroes, even of the thunderer Zeus: "that I speak as the heart in my breast commands". To be able to speak as the heart in my breast commands me is the language of the Gods, and every mortal should endeavour to draw this language of the heart into the light.

Do not abandon us. Write to us again soon. We are curious on the behaviour of your rationalist. With him you have also spoken of how the heart in the breast commands, otherwise he would have never let himself into the tests. — We give our regards, etc.

Doctor to the Deacon

In your letter you have shown me that the genius in you is moving its wings. I rejoice over that as sincerely as if I married and bore myself a child. Stir and move only heartily amongst each other, that will give the young wings of genius strength, and it will soon strive for the clouds.

My rationalist has done nicely. I did not see him for eight days. I made the assumption in the end that he might have left M...t in order to not come into further contact with me. Finally I saw him again on the usual path and set out at once to meet him. He saw me already from a distance, as if he had been waiting for me. I went up to him, greeted him, and he at once began to report to me about the successes of our conversation and his exercises. — "I was", he said, "when I recently left you, in a complete frenzy where I could not say whether I was a deceiver, a deceived, an honourable or a bad man. You gave me tests. I would have to lie if I wanted to tell you they had seemed important to me; regardless of which I was seized because it revolved around whether I have previously been wandering in darkness and been violently enraging myself against the point of my existence. Then the adage occurred to me: practice makes the master; and since we must also consider our life as an art, and every art can only be learnt by practice, I began imagining all possible objects and areas of creation, and became aware distinctly that, as soon as I sent my thoughts directly into the heights, my head was agitated in an unpleasant, almost painful way, by contrast whereas, if I took horizontal objects or objects lying below me into my imagination, I felt in part peaceful, in part strengthening effects. Since I had resolved finally to grow naturally from below upwards, I occupied myself with tree roots, foundations, and my antipodeans in the other hemisphere. This had the result that I seemed as if I were walking in water. — What is that? — You have led me into the labyrinth, you must also help me out again."

Me: "From this labyrinth, you alone can help yourself."
Him: "In what way?"

Me: "Through continuing that which you have started. The spiritual powers felt by you work chaotically to start with, then they grow and develop to a specific activity where you will learn to see their truth and importance."

Him: "But the matter is so new and unusual that one finds an interpretation neither in the history of the present, nor of the past."

Me: "Anyone who seeks interpretations finds such; but someone who goes out of the way and declares it all for nonsense in advance can see none."

Him: "Tell me just *one* example."

Me: "Christ said to Peter at the washing of the feet: He that is washed needeth not save to wash his feet, but is clean every whit*."

Him: "And you are of the view that this foot washing refers to something of the sort?"

Me: "To what else then?"

Him: "To a moral purification."

Me: "The limited, the orthodox seek everywhere for morals, the free thinker everywhere for nature."

Him: "As a result the Bible would not be an untruthful book?"

Me: "It is the book of the unveiled spiritual powers of human nature."

Him: "Why do we not look in our times anymore for such unveiled powers?"

Me: "Because in the Bible itself no teaching for such an unveiling is contained."

Him: "Then the Bible though is an incomplete book!"

Me: "In respect to the teaching, yes; with reference to the effectiveness of the developed powers, divine."

Him: "Why is the teaching lacking?"

Me: "Either one found it to be good to not incorporate it, or it had already been lost."

Him: "And is still lost?"

Me: "Among very few is it still present."

Him: "And these few?"

---

* [Tr.: John 13:10.]

Me: "Do not want to have the persecution of the clergy and the rationalists released on them."

Him: "The matter, as you practice it, is purely rational."

Me: "I think so too. But ask others, and you will hear with what names one can be honoured."

Him: "You must not shy from mockery and danger for the truth."

Me: "You are right, as soon as favourable results are to be foreseen. In the other case you must consult prudence."

Him: "Do you always do that?"

Me: "I do not know. I do, to cite Homer, what the heart in my breast commands."

The man was visibly taken by these words and was already half willing to offer his hand to me in farewell, only his heart was still too distant for him to have to obey its voice.

The next morning I received a letter from him in which he told me he was forced to leave M...t and could therefore not see me again so soon. He gave his address, with the request of entering into an exchange of letters with me and being permitted to visit me in the capital. He seems to be a talented, energetic man, and to the extent that we succeed in winning him over to the higher truth, much will have been done for the matter.

I know of nothing to say to you but to demand you and your friends provide the language of the heart, of the disposition, of the form, of the genius, in one word, the language of the spirit with more and more air.

We breathe in air, but we also breathe in spirit. We want to deal with this chapter when I will be amongst you again. Until then, take care! — Give my regards to our friends and tell them I am with sincere regards always bound with them in spirit, etc.

Of the Doctor's Return

The Doctor had returned again to the city. His friends gave him a small party in the house of the Professor, whereby they expressed their joy at having him back again. He felt deeply stirred by the sincere evidence of their love and expressed this in a way that you could consider to be one of his instructive lectures. The Professor expressed himself over it openly, when he said, "The good Doctor has shown us today more than ever what it means to speak as the heart in the breast commands. According to his words all that we feel and express with words is nourishment for the spirit. — It is also true what he said, there is nothing purer and more dispassionate than the feeling of joy amongst sincere friends. We enjoy this pleasure today in its fullest expression, and if he claims though that the greater part belongs to him, we can concede such only in some respect in so much as he is riper for the goodness and therefore possesses the ability to feel also in a more unspoilt way. Meanwhile we are his match today in that with the feelings of our joy that of thanks is joined and rises to the highest level."

The two other friends approved of the Professor's words and made a toast to the Doctor which again penetrated from full hearts to his heart. The Doctor responded to this outpouring of hearts with a few moving words and then said, "Now enough. I am curious about the story with the Dean, whether he is giving it a rest, and what the consistory has said to his petition."

The Doctor had, before he went into the countryside, at the request of the consistory provided a defence against the Dean which was so succinct that the former had only to consult about the form to declare the Dean's complaint to be inadmissible and to reject it. Wehrmann was informed of this and, since he could expect nothing further, declared himself to be completely satisfied. — The Professor, who had a few trusted acquaintances in the consistory, gave news of the impression which Wehrmann's essays had made with them, and that a few of the members expressed themselves entirely for his views and one shall even have expressed himself as follows.

It was regrettable to not be permitted to publish these essays in that in them reason and the word of God were thus connected so that you could not separate them anymore. The rationalists have only one support — reason; the orthodox also only one — blind faith; the edifice of the accused though rests on two columns of which you can dispense with neither, provided that you shall not walk uncertainly on crutches.

— Another spoke as follows.

Doctor Wehrmann's ideas seem to him to be the transition into a new age which must follow by necessity should the religion not perish. — The word of God or prophecy as a gift of humanity occurs to him to be so natural that he had to only be amazed to hear it for the first time. Through that alone Christianity remains in its divine dignity without doing violence to reason and stimulating it constantly to resistance.

A few spoke in this way and offered in addition that since Doctor Wehrmann was not expressing his views in schools and from pulpits, but rather as a scholar, a petition against him could not take place and therefore could not be heeded. There was certainly also a few who did not declare themselves in agreement with the above and even claimed that, to the extent one led religion back to the basis of nature, it was robbed of its divine adornment and made into a playground of logical disputations and sophistries. — As varied as the views were, however, the unanimous conclusion was given to reject the petition of the Dean and to make known to him the disapproval of his actions and his intolerance.

Those present thanked the Professor for sharing this report, rejoiced over it, and expressed themselves openly in praise of the consistory. — Wehrmann said, "The consistory has done what it could do and had to do. It is more conducive to it to reprimand its subordinates than to compromise itself externally, which would have happened without further ado had it taken sides with the fanaticism of the Dean and opened amongst themselves a refuge for intolerance. Hence they deserve praise because they have recognised their position and claimed the dignity for themselves."

It was now arranged to inform the three clergymen who had been selected as judges of the contest of all that had happened. But in order to evade any misunderstandings, it was decided to visit Parson Punter to present it orally to him and to ask him to do the same with the two other clergymen.

The day was already determined for this outing when a new event drew the attentiveness of the friends to itself and hindered them in it.

The government physician Borndach, doctor and friend of the Dean Blumhof, was informed by the latter of everything, and since he did not know what he should think about the Doctor, he decided to make his acquaintance, and hence turned in writing to the Assessor whom he had already known for a long time from the house of the Dean. — When the Doctor was made familiar with this plan, he immediately agreed to it, and tasked the Assessor with asking the government physician in writing when and where it suited him to appear in order to get to know him face to face. The latter gave answer in a roundabout way and reported that he would await the Doctor on the following Sunday in B...l, a village halfway between his place of residence and the capital, in the tavern The Eagle.

The Simplest Dogma

Sunday came. The three friends had asked the doctor for permission to accompany him, and thus they travelled in the most glorious weather from his house and arrived at B...l, just as the people were leaving the church. The Professor knew the local parson and felt urged to make a visit on him in order to renew the previous acquaintance again. He revealed this wish to his companions, who all approved, but the Doctor added, "We will accompany you."

They arrived at the Parson's, who expressed a great joy at seeing the Professor again after a long time. He was introduced to the others, whereby he behaved with such affability and urbanity that one immediately became aware that this was no common village parson. He had wine brought out, drank to a good acquaintanceship, but remarked at the same time to not be like the good Professor and only visit him when other motives draw one here. The visitors responded to this pleasantry with appropriate thanks and promised to take him by his word when he promised them at the same time to also visit them in the city. He gave his promise, the others theirs, and the visit seemed to be ending with the usual forms of politeness when the Professor expressed his regret to the parson over not having come earlier in order to hear him for once at the pulpit in the church. — Notwithstanding these regrets also only being a sort of form of politeness, a conversation though unfolded from it which deserves to be described on account of the principles expressed in it. —

The Parson, Gutmann by name, responded to the words of the Professor as follows.

Gutmann: "You need not regret having come earlier, for I say nothing more at the pulpit than in everyday life."

Professor: "You must though speak with an elevated voice, with a certain priestly unction."

Gutmann: "Not even that, in so far as the simplicity with which I treat the matter tolerates no strange gesticulations."

Professor: "You cannot speak at the pulpit though and behave as in profane life. Indeed, even the content of what is said must be of a select, ordered, and more elevated tendency."

Gutmann: "The parson of a close congregation amongst whose members he lives all week, and also shares then instruction and advice, must wean himself of such external aids if the audience shall have faith in him. Even the content of the sermon must only be a continuation of that which he says to the people at home, by the sick bed, in the fields, and on all occasions of village and domestic life, then one thing connects to another, they see themselves and their business in the content of the sermon just as they find it again in their households."

Professor: "What you are saying is a puzzle to me. I cannot think of such an outcome from any educated audience, much less from country folk."

Gutmann: "Here it all comes down to what you say to the people. If I wanted to unveil to my listeners the secrets of Christianity or the principles of dogma which scholars themselves barely understand, then they would admittedly take home less, even not see in the sermon themselves and their domestic life. Led by this conviction, I have reduced my talks to the simplest Christian principles and say to my congregation at the pulpit and in their houses nothing else but: 'Be industrious! Be peaceable and have trust in God!'" —

The Doctor, whom these words had surprised, fastened his eyes on the Parson as if he wanted to read it in his face. The Professor responded.

Professor: "You will though also teach your listeners knowledge of God?"

Gutmann: "I teach them to trust in God."

Professor: "How might they trust in him, if they do not know him?"

Gutmann: "If they do not know him, then he knows them, and that is sufficient for both."

Professor: "But it would have to be better if both knew each other."

Gutmann: "So suggest your scholars who either do not seek to know him at all or judge him in a human way. I have made according to my various experiences and researches into an inviolable law the teaching of my pastoral children such a firm trust in God as is ever possible, because I have the factual conviction that such a trust does not disgrace and will certainly be rewarded. But here there is no talk of any mystical or pietistic trust, but rather of such a trust that, supported by diligence and a peaceable heart, sees the fingers of God in the home and trusts in his guidance with a thankful demeanour."

Professor: "Where diligence and peace reign, the household must also prosper, and consequently the trust in God becomes nothing more than a religious encore."

Gutmann: "You are still the old man, always inclined to take from humanity their sanctum and to exist with your own powers. With me, in my parish you do not get by with such hypotheses. Diligence and peace might be sufficient to form a domestic circle and to provide it with bread and butter. But when illnesses, poor growth, when moral evil, which often intervenes more deeply in family life than one suspects, when temptation and seduction arrive, then nobody but God can help. And I invite you to go house to house in the parish, and you will find none where infallible evidence of a reward for steady faith would not show itself."

The Doctor, who up to then had not spoken a word, stood up from his armchair and said, "It would be worth the effort though to walk around the village a little and, even if not seeing the kitchens of the residents, at least the front doors which are always a sign of the inner arrangement." They agreed to this suggestion and went with the Parson on a round through the village. What they saw indicated cleanliness and order. Everyone expressed their contentment, only the Professor, who had not yet mastered all the evil spirits in himself, would have liked to also see the inside of one of the houses and speak to its inhabitants. — The Parson responded to such an utterance, "Go to any house you like; you will find the same attitude everywhere." — The Professor chose for his intentions one which was not the largest, but also did not belong amongst the quite small ones, and entered with the entire group. The inhabitants were very surprised to receive at once such a numerous and august visit. When they saw the

Parson amongst them though, they plucked up courage and made the gentlemen welcome with the request to take a seat on the chairs and benches. The Professor considered himself to be the spokesman and said, "We do not want to be a burden for long and are merely here in order to say to you that your good Parson has the prospect of a better parish and he will soon leave you." — "God will prevent that," the lady of the house said in shock. The man said, "That the good Parson won't do; for he knows how we have need of him here. Other parishes might bring in more money, but he will not harvest more love than amongst us anywhere else. And as far as the money is concerned, he should say how much less he has with us than there, and we will replace it doubled from our own means." — After this the lady of the house again took up the conversation and said, "No, dear Parson, you must not leave. You have made us all too much into your children that you could leave us. — Remember still the time when you arrived here, how poor and disreputable our village was. You did not meet any peaceable families, not a house that was not in debt; no Sunday or festival passed without a drinking spree and fights as if the entire village were in uproar. Then you came, dear Parson, like an angel from heaven. — You made us into humans through instruction and example. You have impressed trust in God and given to us the proof yourself that God is near to us and helps when we trust him. — Do you still recall the time when my husband lay on his deathbed? — Everyone, even the doctor gave up on him; you alone called on me to not let my faith fall, to give him into the hands of God. I trusted, he himself still kept faith in your words, and see here, God helped. — The gentlemen will encounter such mindsets and examples in every house, rich or poor, among us, and hence I know in advance the good Parson cannot leave us and disgrace our trust in him." — The Parson stood up modestly stirred and said, "Don't worry, good people, I am not leaving you. Amongst you the seed which I am called on to sow bore the first fruits; and am I now supposed to leave such a fertile field? — The gentleman here wanted only to try you, because he doubted whether I also had enough standing and authority to head such a large congregation." —

The Simplest Dogma

Here the man of the house again stepped forward and replied, "Whether our dear Parson possesses enough standing and authority to head us! — He does not head us; he loves us. — He does not command us; he leads the way by example. We do not ever have to seek him, he is there when advice and help is needed. — In the fields, on the street, on all the paths he belongs to us just as well as in the school and in the church. — God is with him, for his nearness brings blessings. He is a servant of God not only in word, but also in deed, because he connects us with God and shows us his fingers in all affairs. In this way he is not only ours, we are also his and will stay with each other as long as God preserves him for us."

"Amen!", said the Doctor. — "Here there are no more words to be added. To the contrary, I promise the good people that, in the event the city ever shall not tolerate me anymore, I will move here and will place myself under the trusting regimen of your worthy Parson."

They left this abode and went through a crossroads up through the village. Along the way the Professor asked the Parson how he got by with the consistory with his almost dogma-less system. The Parson responded, "The consistory cannot attack my system because I derive it from the gospels and support it with as many citations as they desire. Certainly I have created the system not from the Bible, but rather from myself. — The Bible is too full of substance — the essential and that fitting for humanity is quite hard to extract, and therefore I asked myself: what is the most beneficial for humanity? And there it resulted in the answer: to live peaceably and without worries over nourishment. — By what is this state obtained? — By diligence and by the help of God. The last point I busied myself with the most of course; but I found that it must realise itself if my religious system should obtain strength. I heard so much about the blessings of God and of the rewards of a childish trust that, where I just found entry, I made inquiries in order to create a clear idea for myself about the evidence for such blessings. I met families who were quite wealthy but sank by and by into the deepest poverty. By contrast I got to know families who possessed nothing, but every day found their earnings as if an invisible hand were caring for them. As soon as I investigated afterwards, it resulted that the first trusted only in themselves and not in God; but the others placed their fate in the hands of him who also feeds the ravens. This evidence was indeed not yet of the sort to found a formal religious system on it, however convincing enough to undertake a test. — I arrived at the local, entirely depraved parish and decided to put my idea into practice, because it, even in the case of failure, could not hurt. But surely for me and this place, it has stood the test; the blessings came and grew with the trust so visibly that not only I, but the entire congregation would vouch for the truth of a divine blessing.

I have said already and shown to you here that I did not create the system of my process from the Bible, but have found it again in the Bible. This then gave me doubled assurance in that both the success and the canonical law spoke for me. For this reason it was easy for me to stroll the path of the strictest liturgy and to be certain of the applause of the consistory who also took my part to such an extent that they wanted to lift me from my current place and provide me with an important city parish. The reason I rejected such an offer, you have already heard. Here I have founded a church; whether it would be possible for me in a larger place is very doubtful. Here I have learn to recognise the nearness of God, and hence I consider my parish to be a sanctum which I believe I am not permitted to leave without sinning."

The Doctor, who up to then had observed a sort of neutrality, thanked the Parson for his accommodating behaviour and for the openness with which he unfolded the system of his approach. — "I admire you, not only on account of the manner of instruction, but also on account of the courage with which you bring it into practice. Many a man would certainly have achieved good things if he had been in a position to unite courage and cleverness properly. Anyone who does not speak the truth from lack of courage is not worthy of it; but anyone who does not use the proper cleverness to be permitted to say it under various, often provided forms is also not worthy of it. — You have known how to adapt your system to the rites to which you are bound, through that you have exalted the rites and served humanity. Hence accept our thanks with the assurance of our honest admiration."

The Simplest Dogma

Modesty did not permit the Parson to answer these thanks properly. He merely said, "The duty of every human is to strive for truth; to a few it is begrudged to take care of themselves, but others must glean for the rest. I belong to the latter — hence my system should be too simple, it comes about thus because I had simple listeners and myself alone to take care of." — The Doctor replied, "You have gleaned splendidly! Unfortunately we must often, blinded by the dust of schooling and self-cleverness, clean our eyes again through scientific inquiries; but anyone who has unspoilt eyes needs no artificial eye-lotion to see the nearness of God. — Thank you for your honesty and be assured that I count your acquaintance amongst the fortunate events of my life."

They took their leave of the Parson, went to the tavern where the Physician had already arrived and greeted the Assessor from the window. When the latter had entered the room with the Doctor and his friends, he introduced the Physician to the former. — The Physician said to the Doctor, "A strange reason brings us into a personal acquaintance which hopefully will turn out to be mutually satisfying. But you are not alone, as I see." — Wehrmann responded, "These are my seconds, but they are so neutral that they will remain at ease even if we should both end up at loggerheads." — The Physician replied, "I hope that it will not come to that." — The Doctor said, "I not only hope, but am certain it won't. But now I ask whether we will begin our debate straightaway or want to wait until we have strengthened ourselves properly by having lunch." — The Physician replied that he had already visited over twenty patients that day, had travelled there, and hence found it more expedient to wait until lunch had been eaten. — Wehrmann was content with that. The meal was brought out, consumed with good appetite, and accompanied by conversation over the latest news, railways, customs affairs, and finally also literature. After the dishes were removed and some dessert had been placed on the table, the Doctor said to the waiter, "We want to be alone and undisturbed now and will ring if we need anything."

***

The Cataract

When they were alone, the Physician began, "You have gotten caught up in a conflict with one of my friends, the Dean Blumhof, which I am willing to settle if the views are not at all too opposed to each other. — You see in me the Dean's doctor who is obligated to take care not only of the health of his body, but also of his soul, without which the physical health will not last long. Here, the good Assessor is his nearest blood relative. As easily as the Dean believed himself able to ignore to start with a hostile position towards the latter, he is not master of his feelings; and if here an amicable relationship is not to be reestablished, then it is feared that an incurable melancholy will overpower him and send him to a sickbed. — He was accustomed on the first Sunday of the month to seeing the Assessor, and occasionally his wife and children, visit and recall old times. Now this first Sunday is a day of mourning for him, and he often says that most of his relatives are dead and those who still live abandon him and sacrifice him for strangers. — You see thus that help is needed. I cannot give it, the Assessor does not want to give it, you are thus alone the man who is in a state to step in here effectively by giving up the Assessor and delivering him to his uncle, or putting yourself on a footing with the uncle where the Assessor can treat the Dean as his uncle, but you as a friend." —

The Doctor said to this, "Over the first matter, my friend, the good Assessor, has to decide. The second can resolve itself as soon as the Dean makes the effort to get to know me more closely."

Physician: "Allow me to speak openly. The Dean is of the view that in your company his nephew is in a den of iniquity. I have taken it upon myself to investigate this den and to treat my patient according to the result."

Doctor: "You thus want to feel my pulse then! — It will please me if you find the vein which can inform you."

Physician: "I will certainly find the pulse, provided that the arm is kept at ease."

Doctor: "I will hold my arm still. Feel it!"

Physician: "Good, then I ask, to which of the thousands of sects of Christianity do you belong?"

Doctor: "To none."

Physician: "Thus you are forming your own?"

Doctor: "Not even that."

Physician: "Then you are in the end not a Christian?"

Doctor: "Over that the Assessor shall give evidence."

Assessor: "The good Doctor is a Christian as all should be who call themselves Christians."

Physician: "Eh, then let's hear what his distinction consists of."

Assessor: "He believes in God and in his word through Christ."

Physician: "I believe that too and so does my friend, the Dean."

Doctor: "Then we are indeed agreed."

Physician: "Not entirely. There must be some hook which my friend cannot loosen and hence considers his nephew for lost. What is this hook?"

Doctor: "The Dean believes in direct, arbitrary influence of God, in a word, in miracles, whilst I explain everything according to the laws of nature."

Physician: "That is a lot. Sir, to the extent you are in a position to do that, I will also swear to your standard and stand immediately for my friend."

Doctor: "I do not know how I shall be able provide some light for you over it in such a short time. — Nature is everything. Something that wasn't in it is unimaginable. But now the limited mind of humans sought in a way to help itself and placed God far above nature. As soon as this had happened, it could not fail that another party would appear and say, 'If God is above nature, then the devil and hell are below it'. — Now we stand here and have three worlds: a heaven (God), a hell (the devil), and finally nature. Since such a division must appear to any rational person to be utter nonsense, I altered the principle and said God and nature are only one thing; it through him and he in it. Supported by this principle, I succeeded in solving the seeming puzzles of the Bible and explaining them better than the Dean with all his adherents."

Physician: "I do not yet understand you. What you are saying sounds so materialistic that you can arrive at the suspicion that you let God arise out of nature just as much as nature out of God."

Doctor: "God is the purest thing in nature, nature the coarser part of God and hence both are only one thing."

Physician: "Now, and the result of this implication?"

Doctor: "Is that humanity, a child of nature, is also a child of God, consequently would have to be only one thing with God and nature."

Physician: "But how does Christ fit into this unity?"

Doctor: "Thus that he could not have occurred without such a unity."

Physician: "I don't understand that."

Doctor: "Then you are just as prejudiced as the Dean."

Physician: "I am not prejudiced, and do not want to be. My office, my craft does not allow it. I must go the way of nature and cannot believe in it at all if I do not find God in it."

Doctor: "Your official nature is a small branch of a stem which is rooted in eternity and towers into eternity."

Physician: "I can seek out the trunk from the branch."

Doctor: "To the extent you do that, good for you. Only I doubt it."

Physician: "What gives you cause to doubt?"

Doctor: "The weakness of human nature which far too easily falls in love with the branch."

Physician: "What, you consider that I too — —"

Doctor: "I consider that the Physician very often stands above the man."

Physician: "From what do you conclude that?"

Doctor: "Because you do not know where Christ comes from, and where you should place him."

Physician: "I place him amongst humanity."

Doctor: "But as what?"

Physician: "That I do not know how to say if I do not want to use the Dean's words."

Doctor: "And do you not give them sufficient credence?"

Physician: "I must confess, no. — Would you not like to answer in my name for once?"

Doctor: "Christ stands in nature as a human. But he stands also in God because he is God and human at the same time. His person is human; his spirit is God. Through the person he was visible to humanity; but he reveals his spirit through the living spiritual word which flows from his pure divinity. Thus he represents as human the word which is God, and announces it to humanity. His word, his spirit, however, is the eternal Christ. This he wants to give to us, and thus we take it in, thus he has become flesh in us and will deliver us from sin and death. — The person of Christ cannot enter into us, but the spirit can. This spirit, however, did not first become flesh with Christ, but rather stems from eternity and will also be in eternity."

Physician: "Dear Doctor, those are sentences which sound magnificent, indeed divine, but reveal nothing to me."

Doctor: "Do you believe in a revelation of God?"

Physician: "Yes, through his works."

Doctor: "The outer senses see the shell of his works, but do not perceive the spirit. Do you not believe in revelation through the word?"

Physician: "Sometimes I believe, and sometimes not."

Doctor: "Why do you sometimes not believe?"

Physician: "Because I consider such a direct communication to be impossible."

Doctor: "Why do you consider such to be impossible? — Because you are overcome by the delusions of orthodoxy and think God must, in order to speak to humans, climb down in high majesty from heaven and enter into conversation with them. But to the extent that God himself, that is, his spirit, resides in us, to the extent being able to hear the voice of the spirit and to turn towards it is a natural gift of humanity, the matter obtains a natural form, and we have to ascribe it to ourselves if we constantly remain children in the most important affair of life."

Physician: "What? You are claiming such a voice lies in every human, and each bears the gift in themselves of becoming a prophet?"

The Cataract

Doctor: "I claim that with such certainty as I can say that every healthy human child is capable of learning to count to five."

Physician: "Dear Doctor! I feel like a blind man who sits under the knife of the operator and waits expectantly for the latter to cut away the cataract and open the eye to the light. Cut at once."

Doctor: "I have already cut, but the cataract is too thick."

Physician: "Then cut once more."

Doctor: "Pay attention, I am cutting. — To the extent the history of the world encloses no divine revelation through the word, it is a farce in which the greatest men and geniuses stride across the stage as theatrical heroes and await fearfully whether anyone will call out applause. — But if the earlier times received divine revelations through the word, then the races living now must also be able to receive them, if God shall be wise, just, full of love, and eternal. The ability to talk with God is the living Christ within us. The goal of his religion, however, consists of connecting us by means of the word with God and raising us to him. Anyone who feels, thinks, teaches, and speaks otherwise is no Christian, to the contrary, he acts directly against Christian principles and will also never be permitted to enter into the residences which the father has promised to all the true confessors of the word which Christ teaches us."

Physician: "Doctor, I believe the cataract is gone, but my eyes still hurt."

Doctor: "There you must bind them for a short time in order to give them rest in which to recover. — Dear Assessor, ring so that champagne can be brought!"

The Physician looked at the Doctor with such wonderment, as if the cataract had been taken from his eyes, and as if he had seen a ray of light after a long night. — The champagne was brought, and the Assessor poured it. The Doctor first presented it to the Physician and then to the others. He himself took the last glass, clinked it with the Physician and said, "To good results from the operation you've survived." — The Physician emptied his glass, and said, still holding it in his hand, "I would rather have believed in the humanity of Mehmed Ali than to find in you such a doctor. But I rejoice that it is you, and I will pester the Dean diligently in order to make his cataract ripe for the operation." — Everybody now drank to the health of the Physician, and since the waiter had already left again, he took the lead and said, "My good Doctor! I have a short while ago let you feel and touch me to your heart's content, and confess you have not operated poorly. Only so many ideas are swirling around in my head still which leave a gap in your system of operation and which, if it is possible for you, I beg you to fill in. — According to your view the human is a born prophet, and if he does not know this gift, then we have to ascribe our distance from nature and our indolence not to it, but rather to our wrongheadedness. Now I say, even if the individual or even entire corporations might be led so far from the path, a disposition cannot be so entirely lost that no traces were to be seen of it at all. Consequently though your glorious sentences remain hypotheses which could be true, but also could not be true. I am a doctor and appraise the psyche only when I can look at it physically as well, that is, in its visible effects. — According to which principles do you want to continue to treat me in order to provide me bright light in such a realm of hypotheses?"

Doctor: "In this case I leave myself to you and your experiences. No mortal has so frequent opportunity to see the freedom of the psyche as the doctor. Any doctor, and even if he only has the tiniest practice, must have had experiences at the beds of his patients which no logic can explain. — It has happened to you already more than once that a patient, whose illness you did not consider to be dangerous, foresaw death with certainty and even gave the day and hour of it. But unfortunately I have to say that doctors do not pay attention to such gifts, and when they are asked about it, evade with the answer that it is certainly strange — an innate play of fate — and thereby cut off the paths to a thorough investigation. And why? Because they do not possess the courage and the honesty to draw into the realm of positive phenomena and investigations facts over which any joker could make remarks and belittle the practice."

Physician: "I know where you are headed. The condition of the somnambulist certainly delivers phenomena which is not to be explained, and therefore it has already gone out of style.

The Cataract

When patients in their last days commit such abnormalities, the doctor cannot make allowances for them, cannot draw conclusions from them if he does not want to deny all faith in rationality and put himself amongst the ranks of despised dreamers."

Doctor: "In order to not be put in the said realm, in order to give jokers no opportunity to exercise their sarcasm on us, we let a field lie fallow on which the most precious fruits of truth are to be drawn. — Is that right? Is that manly? — As long as you have an authority for yourself; as long as you can call on Mesmer and others, then you can have courage because you can in need place the authority in front and have it battle for us. But as soon as it concerns acting yourself, even looking nature in the eye, then we are cowardly and weak and would rather let everything perish than have a stain be attached to us by some idiots. — Somnambulism is an unfree, a bound state in which a blindman would like to use the eyes of another to see the truth. Already by the former being blind no light can illuminate him. And if you consider entirely that the the mesmerised person usually passes into the mental state of mind of the mesmeriser, then nothing at all is to be expected. — With the patient on the sick bed it is quite different. Here there is a free state. Everything which the world, which the passions attach to the human flees in such a state, and the human has nothing more than themselves, than that part which is directly connected with the eternal spirit of creation. In such moments the mist disappears for a time, the doors to eternity open, and the human sees by means of his natural gift the few hours of his life as if in a mirror before himself. — In this I call on you; you can give testimony to what I've said. The doctor is a priest of the body, the clergyman a priest of the soul. The doctor must make the body healthy so that the clergyman can act on the soul. To the clergyman lies whether the evil is to be removed from the soul so that the doctor becomes master of the body. In this way a relationship arises where doctor and priest go hand in hand and can work for the health of both the body and the soul. — As priests and doctors now stand, they are two beings who never touch one another and see each other as a sort of non-human. From physics, psychology must be learnt and from psychology physics, then the form is spiritualised and from the form the phoenix of life rises to heaven. — This as a salve on your still weak eye. And now yet another toast: long live the Dean who loves his nephew and would like to reconcile with him!" — "Long live the Dean!", they all agreed.

After this the Physician once more took the lead and said, "Doctor! I bore the desire to get to know you personally. You gratified my wish; thank you. Whether I know you better than before after seeing you, I do not know, for it seems to me as if a chasm lies between us which I will never be capable of crossing. I, as doctor, should have no other teacher but nature; in your vicinity I seem to myself to be a common school pedant who, without written citations, without the authority of precedent, does not possesses a mustard seed of knowledge, while you stand there as if you had seen everything with your own eyes and tested everything with your own senses. Science, art, and religion are to you just *one* field on which the types of fruit of these three realms alternate according to your free will, indeed, so that you can pluck this one at this moment and another in the following. To the extent it is possible, teach me this art, and you shall find a thankful student in me. For proof of my serious intentions I promise you as a test to take on the Dean, to break the horns of his rigid orthodoxy, and to make him, even if not a student of your views, at least into a tolerant supporter. — But now farewell! Visit me when and for as long as you want. The Assessor can testify to you that one lives quite well in my house. I count on seeing you quite soon and for a long time at my place. And now to my patients."

Commands were given to harness the horses and bring the bill. When everything was sorted, they parted with the mutual assurance of having spent an important day together.

Everyone arrived home safe and well. The Physician in order to visit a number of patients, the others in order to impress on their memories what they had heard that day and to use it as a foundation for new investigations. The Doctor rejoiced over the day mainly on account of the Assessor whom he hoped prospectively to reconcile with his uncle.

***

First Attack

The Physician arrived home, full of the impressions of the day, and hurried to visit his patients in order to then recapitulate at home and note in his diary what he had heard. The main thing indeed which behoved him was to report to the Dean the outcome of his meeting with the Doctor and to prepare him for a reconciliation with the Assessor. But he put off his visit in order to prepare himself appropriately and to properly take it to him on the following day should he be too pig-headed.

The next day he went before lunch to the Dean who was expecting him impatiently. The Physician presented his report, told him how delighted he had been, and that Doctor Wehrmann was not so evil a man as the Dean had described him. The latter remarked straightaway that his advocate had deserted him and been won over by the Doctor. He called out half morosely, half wistfully, "What magic this man has that he makes all hearts which usually adhered to me turn away from me!" — The Physician replied, "The entire magic which he possesses consists of that he is brighter than we are, and not caught up in any prejudices. He sees each thing as it is, and not as we desire that it should be. — When he speaks about Christ, he describes him with such natural and lively colours and contours that reason and feeling tell us immediately, 'that he is'. — When I consider by contrast our dogmatic Christ, twisted by Pietists, forced into mystical forms by the rationalists, it seems to me as if you were playing with soap bubbles which vanish as soon as you want to inspect them. His Christ has stability and power; he exists and will exist, and even if the name should be lost. And this image lives in nature, resides in the hearts of humanity and gives them strength to enter into the realm of the father where Christ reigns through the spirit of eternal truth."

"What does my nephew say?", the Dean asked after this. — "Your nephew," the Physician replied, "rejoices in the hope of seeing you again soon. We drank to your health with full glasses, in the certain outlook that you will soon support us." — "That must surely be carefully considered beforehand," the Dean suggested. — The Physician, however, replied that where the hearts speak, it must not be considered for long. "I will tell you," he continued, "some other time everything which was said, as faithfully as I can, and if your heart is not entirely covered by the dust of school, then it must break through the crust and prepare for you more happy days with the love of your nephew, and in the consciousness of having found worthy men and friends." — "Don't hope for too much," the Dean replied. The other man said, "I know what I am about, and hence enough for today. Tomorrow I will see you again and will take your pulse as doctor of body and soul, and prescribe the means which I consider necessary."

He left. But the Dean sighed and said to himself, "The men want to leave the paved road and build another! Will it surely be possible?"

***

Orthodoxy

The Physician was a man of sound heart and mind, and therefore the views of the Doctor, which united the temporal with the eternal in a natural way, found easy acceptance with him. He expressed himself so clearly over them in his diary that it will certainly be interesting to everyone to hear his conclusions over them. We extract from it thus an article which he wrote over orthodoxy, and present it word for word here.

"There are truths which are irrevocable and eternal, but also such as only belong to certain circumstances, specific times and natures. The first are the purely philosophical and religious, but the others agree with the passing needs and appearances. The forms of logic and numbers are eternal; but that which we discuss through logic or calculate with numbers can be temporarily true, often even only for a few moments. For example, that two times two is four will remain true for all eternity; but that two times two guilders will forever make 240 kreuzers* is uncertain, because you can make the guilders smaller or larger, can even alter them for certain regions. Such simple examples can, if we think without bias, give us information about the nature of orthodoxy. Anyone who claims two times two are four is right for all eternity; but anyone who, proceeding from this truth, concludes that because two times two is four, two times two guilders must also make up 240 kreuzers for all eternity, they are orthodox and will become all the more intolerant, the more they defend their view. When we apply this to the Christian religion, we must consider it to be apodictic truth when you say the spirit of Christ is eternal and will remain eternal. If we wanted to also claim this of his person, then you enter

---

*   [Tr.: kreuzers and guilders are old German units of currency.]

into a labyrinth of hypotheses where you would have to go from one state of confusion to another."

From this we see how thoroughly the Physician prepared himself, and in what way he intended to open the attempt at converting the Dean. He visited him from then on every day, sought in every way to make the breach in order to penetrate into the well-defended fortress. Only for a long time he did not get any nearer to his goal, to the contrary there were often stormy scenes where both parties were driven further apart than ever.

The Physician gave the Assessor from time to time news of his fruitless endeavours; finally he shared with him a conversation between him and the Dean from which finally the desired result emerged.

"I arrived," thus the letter went, "yesterday morning at ten o'clock at your uncle's and was resolved not to leave again until he gave his word to agree to a meeting with you and the Doctor in my presence. — I began on my entry to his study in the following way:

Me: 'Good morning, Dean!'

Him: 'Good morning.'

Me: 'Slept well?'

Him: 'Quite well.'

Me: 'Did not have any bad dreams?'

Him: 'I dreamt of you.'

Me: 'And how did I appear to you? Perhaps with a flaming sword?'

Him: 'No, not so impressively. You appeared to me as a small man who was endeavouring to carry me over a ditch.'

Me: 'And did I carry you over?'

Him: 'No. You were too weak for it.'

Me: 'Then I will have been required to look for a helper?'

Him: 'Yes, you ran away to fetch one.'

Me: 'And did one then come?'

Him: 'No, I awoke before you appeared again.'

Me: 'That is good. In this way I am superfluous and need not endeavour further in reconciling you with your nephew.'

Him: 'To the extent this can happen without the Doctor, I am ready in every way.'

Me: 'At all events to also meet him once at the Assessor's?'

Him: 'That would be extremely irksome to me.'

Me: 'And yet I do not see how a radical reconciliation is possible without this.'

Him: 'My nephew should give in, should consider that I am the elder, the brighter one, then he may visit the Doctor as often as he likes; only I do not want to see him.'

Me: 'That won't work. Such a process conflicts with the love of humanity which a clergyman, a dean, must never harm.'

Him: 'I love the just; the unjust I cannot hamper on the path of ruin.'

Me: 'Where is the path of ruin? Are you certain that the Doctor wanders on it and not you?'

Him: 'Yes.'

Me: 'What evidence have you of that?'

Him: 'The Bible.'

Me: 'The Doctor understands the Bible as well as the theologians who are already entangled in prejudice before they are capable even of thinking.'

Him: 'I am free of prejudices and follow the letter of the law without allowing myself to be led astray.'

Me: 'The letter of each of those laws is dead; the spirit brings it to life. You claim Christianity is present as principle of creation in nature, in that God at the very beginning already saw he had to create angels who would fall away from him in order to have sinful humans emerge from the corrupt regions who would be needful of a saviour, who could be no other than the son sprung from God. — Dear Dean! If this system which you want to burden us with is not utter nonsense, indeed, unworthy of an almighty God, then I do not know anymore what one should call confusion. Give me any day the Doctor's theory which makes no mention of fallen angels, but rather claims that the spirit, the word, and the life which Christ taught is the true Christ who was there before Abraham was, and will be until the end of all days. These are views which a sound human understanding can still digest. The fallen angels which according to your account must be created for the fall in order to create sinful humans are neither for the heart, nor for the mind the slightest nourishment, to the contrary we must regret the poor fallen angels, now poor devils, on whose damnation we founded our sinful lives.'

Him: 'Dear Physician, you bring me to despair! — I should tear down an edifice which I erected with effort, maintained with care, in which I find ease for the here and now and the hereafter? That is asking for too much. Do not expect a friend to leave the safe residence and live in a rotten hut which can collapse at any time.'

Me: 'Your residence offers you no security because it rests on loose foundations. Therefore come and leave such! Do not push away friends who talk honestly with you and offer you a safe haven for the days of need.'

Him: 'I can't.'

Me: 'Good, then farewell! — I do not want to be the friend any longer of a man who denies love of humanity because of a confused system, blocks his ears from truth, and knows in a vain dean's pride nothing else but his opinion, and is a greater high priest than any the history of more bigoted times ever shows.'

Him: 'Dear Physician, you forget with whom you are speaking.'

Me: 'No, I do not forget and will never forget that when you through your severity distanced everyone from yourself, I remained loyal to you from consideration of your otherwise splendid qualities. But now, since you esteem the friendship as little as the bonds of blood, I do not see why I should not rather connect with another who possesses tolerance enough to let each see with their own eyes and hear with their own ears, whilst you are stubbornly forcing your perspective on everything in order to assess the objects afterwards through badly polished glasses.'

The Physician departed and left the Dean in the most violent agitation, but he could not bear such a state for long, took his hat and cane, and went to the school in order there to either forget his displeasure or cool down. The schoolmaster knew him too well to not immediately notice that a storm was threatening, and hence evaded the remarks of the Dean so adroitly that the latter had to leave again without having dispatched even *one* lightning bolt. He went quickly from the schoolhouse, and when he wanted to turn around the corner of it, he ran into the Physician who, not expecting anything of the sort, almost fell backwards onto the ground. The latter, who, on account of his good nature, had already recovered again from his displeasure, called out, "Eh, eh, good Dean! Where are you off too so hurriedly in such a storm?"

The Dean responded, 'I am seeking out friends who do not place the chair before the door for me every time.'

Me: 'Then I stand at your service.'

Him: 'You, who would throw away a precious stone out of obstinacy!' —

Me: 'Dean, you are a precious stone, but despite your dean's dignity still a rough precious stone.'

Him: 'When I talk of a precious stone, I do not mean myself, but rather the matter which I champion.'

Me: 'You may mean what you want, you are wrong. Who will get so excited for such a matter?'

Him: 'Who will not get excited for the sake of a good matter?'

Me: 'To see that justice is also done to others is a human duty. Certainly experience teaches that where two get mixed up in each other's work, reason is put aside and judged hostilely.'

Him: 'Who can accuse me of bias?'

Me: 'Not I; but I know from experience that such a meeting affects us fatally. — In the early period of my presence here a doctor sometimes came into this area whom all the world considered to be a man of miracles. As amicably as I greeted him on the street and in company, I was though heartily glad when he was away from here again. It may be thus with you towards the Doctor now, it might have been thus with the priests and scribes towards Christ; but that is of no help! You must vanquish your dislike, must make peace, then you will conquer yourself and show your subordinates that you are worthy to be their leader.'

The Dean responded here with not a syllable; but the Physician continued, 'Come to my house with me. I have opened a bottle of sherry that is excellent. We will empty it to the health of the Doctor.' — 'Go to —', said the Dean, but swallowed the last word. The Physician took him by the arm, led

Johann Baptist Krebs

him away, and brought him finally to understand that he was to see the Doctor and calmly converse with him.

***

Reconciliation

The Physician, who was not the man to defer a project for long, invited the Assessor to get the Doctor to visit him in a few weeks in order in this way to come into contact with the Dean. The Doctor did not agree to this plan, but said, "The Dean can only meet with me in the presence of several others because then his official dignity protects him, and it makes it easy for him to maintain a secure stance. Hence we will travel in the next week to B...g, order from here a good lunch from there by post, invite the Dean and the Physician along with the three parsons who were supposed to have been judges over our contest, and thus the good matter would indeed have no innate power in itself if we should not succeed in effecting a complete reconciliation." — The Assessor undertook with the Physician to make all the appropriate preparations and orders. The Doctor wrote to Parson Punter and tasked him with informing the other two clergymen and inviting them to participate. The Professor requested permission to also be permitted to invite the Parson Gutmann, because the latter, if the two combatants should have to be kept too much apart, would be able to placate everyone by the simplicity of his views, which he undertook to do; only the Physician altered this plan in that the lunch should take place in his house because the participation of the Dean would thereby be made easier and any disturbance could be evaded more safely. — This suggestion found general approval, whilst one assumed the Physician would not place such a burden on himself if he did not feel strong enough to bear it. — The Thursday of the next week was set for the gathering, partly in order to not defer a good thing for too long, and partly to see the Assessor reconciled with his uncle as soon as possible.

The day arrived. At twelve o'clock all the guests from out of town were assembled in the house of the Physician. The Dean was not yet present because the Physician had arranged with him that he would inform him when the meal was ready in order to not embarrass him into conversing with formal compliments. — The Dean approached the house. They looked at him awkwardly. The Physician hurried towards him, let him on entering greet those present only with a few words and led him then into the dining room to the place designated for him. Everybody followed him. They took their seats, and after the soup was presented, the appetite which each seemed to have brought along chased away the tension from the company. Other courses arrived — they praised the kitchen. The waiter also did his duty and released the tongues for friendly words. When this mood was general, the Physician used the moment and proposed a toast to the Dean, in which all those present took an unmistakeable part. This accord did not escape the attention of the Dean, for he responded to the toast with the words, "I arrived amongst you to begin with as a stranger. The accord of your wish for my well-being has chased away this feeling, and I ask all those present to take the assurance from me that I have done and said nothing yet in my life which would not have taken place without good intentions."

This utterance gave the Doctor occasion to speak, and he used it in his peculiar way in that he expressed the intention of the day's visit openly, namely to struggle for his matter without, however, losing for a moment from his view the goal of establishing peace. He began therefore with the following words.

"The good Dean loves his nephew, the nephew his uncle. Where love carries the banner, good consequences cannot fail to appear. I am the obstacle which separates them. It is thus on me to do everything in order to put such things aside, or to show that it is nothing real, but rather only produced by false ideas. Hence I ask the good Dean to tell me with all calm and impartiality what fault he finds in me, and in what respect I might be not only of danger to his nephew, but even ruinous."

The Dean became contemplative at this request. A deep silence reigned. Finally he composed himself and said, "The difference in our religious views is something we have already expressed in writing and handed over to these three gentlemen for judgement. Only I have already had to hear so much about the good Physician that I am prepared in advance to remain in the minority. — This should, however, not hinder anymore a reconciliation with my nephew. Not everyone can walk the same paths. It is not given to everyone to grasp and believe the mysteries of our sublime religion; hence not one word more on this topic. But I believe I have the right to insist that one spare my relatives from false doctrines and not force them to be proselytes of views which are contrary to the spirit of true Christianity."

The Doctor now took up the conversation and said, "Dean, you have spoken befitting words when you showed how much the welfare of your nearest relative lies close to your heart. In our written essays indeed all the differences in our religious principles were expressed, only, as it tends to go with written essays, you can interpret them in the most various ways, and from that often misunderstandings arise which lead to fear and conflict. Now we see ourselves in friendly company, are placed eye to eye opposite one another and can discuss any discrepancies in our views. You do not want to force your convictions on your nephew and desire that others should not do so. What you desire is as proper as you considering those who do not agree to be enemies of the peace and the truth. It is merely about whether I am wrong, whether my views conflict with the spirit of true Christianity. I will here express my thoughts frankly and ask that you gift me your attention for a few minutes.

I have studied theology. Family circumstances have deprived me of this calling. I researched the Bible as a young theologian with earnestness and zeal and was initiated by one of my teachers into the system of the fallen angels, the sinful humanity, and the necessity in the history of creation of the death of the son of God decided for all eternity. I gave every effort to put this system in harmony with my simple human understanding, or at least to learn to believe in it. The former I never achieved; the latter seemed to be realised sometimes, but disappeared with the slightest temptation into a nothingness which made me poorer than I previously was. I then gave myself over to the rationalism which promised humanity an unerring light. But oh, it was not a real light, but rather an artificially produced light which, instead of life's warmth, offered the cold of death. I renounced this ephemeral shimmer, like I previously renounced orthodoxy, and said to myself, I can count and calculate from the power of my own spirit; can judge colours and tones; can distinguish the beautiful from the ugly, good from evil; should no innate power be given to me for the exploration of religious truths? — I found no trace for a long time and was close to despairing in myself and humanity when at once the words of the gospel which I had often read before came to my attention and were thus:

> The kingdom of God cometh not with observation: Neither shall they say, Lo here! or, lo there! for, behold, the kingdom of God is within you.*

Men like to devote themselves to romantic-pietistic ideas. You make the heart into an object and play with its feelings. In such weakness I had enthused for a long time after reading the above words and produced no result. — Heaven is in the heart, hence everything which resides in heaven must also be in it. This though flew like a bolt of lightning through my soul and gave my urge to investigate a definite direction. — Our Father, who art in heaven!† — The heaven in me, the father in heaven, thus also in me, was now just a thought to which I clung in order to never let it go again. The heaven in me, the father in heaven; the son, who is the word of the father, in the father; the spirit, emanating from the father and son, all this in heaven and heaven in me; in this connection I had now a system which, to the extent it is found realised in nature, throws the human back on himself and reveals to him by and by all the secrets of life and the Christian religion.

Now the question arose: what is Christ? — How does his person fit into such a system? — If Christ finds a place here, then his appearance is a natural necessity which bears apodictic truth within itself. The person of Christ, however, what is *it*? — The person of Christ is the bearer of the word of God announced by the prophets and expressed in its highest perfection for humanity. The presence of Christ is infallibility made flesh of a prophetic power as a gift in humans which calls to all confessors of Christianity: only through me to the

---

* [Tr.: Luke 17:20–21. The last line reads in the German of Luther's Bible literally as 'it is in the heart'. Note also for the following discussion that 'kingdom of God' appears in the German as *Himmelreich* = 'kingdom of heaven'.]

† [Tr.: cf. Matthew 6:9 and Luke 11:2.]

Reconciliation

truth, to faith, to the father*, to the spirit, and to the kingdom of heaven! Christ in his person is the sublime prophet who was foretold by prophets, recognised by the light of prophesy, and established as the ideal, that is, as the saviour for all of humanity. The eternal Christ, not bound to the person, is though the word of God which flowed from him, which instructs us to likewise seek this living word in order to go to the father in heaven by means of it. — What is it?, I now asked myself. Is somewhere here an incorrect conclusion? — And does the content of the Bible, both the Old and the New Testaments, not fall apart in this sequence of ideas? — Everything is just one. Even the serpent in paradise resides in the heart and entices us to pluck from the tree of knowledge of good and evil and to trust in the self-cleverness of our existence. Who can vanquish this serpent? — Answer: Christ, the living word of God in us. Who must arise from the dead? Christ, the prophetic power in us which we exchanged and killed for being worldly-wise. — Yes, I asked finally: what is sin? And what is the will of the father? Thy will be done in heaven, thus also as on earth†. — How can the father's will be done on earth? — Answer: also in our hearts, if we place the earthly desires and urges under the will of the father. But in heaven the father's will is done if we seek his word, which is Christ, live in this word, and consider everything which is outside of it as inessential or as a gift. — Thus my system was complete; it was now just missing being put into practice. Time and persistence, unbiased research, and strictly obeying the acknowledged good thing were now the means for awakening the light in me and arriving at the purest knowledge. And look, I succeeded in obtaining the rebirth in the spirit and through it came to the word, to the father, and to heaven. — Anyone who wants to take exception to what I have said, they will take exception, I cannot help them; but anyone who possesses the boldness to test this system and seek practical evidence, they will have to say, the human is in God and God in the human, and for that reason the name of God was prized by human tongues for eternity."

---

* [Tr.: cf. John 14:6.]
† [Tr.: cf. Matthew 6:10 and Luke 11:2.]

Here the Doctor fell silent. A general silence reigned. — Parson Gutmann, who had never heard the Doctor speaking in this way before, felt urged to give air to his feelings, and said, "Thank you, good Doctor, for your instructive, clear, and elevating lecture. Although the richness of its content does not want to quite harmonise with the simplicity of my religious principles, I feel nonetheless greatly obligated to you. For the simple countryman my simplicity may be sufficient, in a certain respect even necessary; for the shepherds, the guides, it is not enough; they should know how to draw everything they teach from the basic principles of the religion and to handle it scientifically, to the extent that they shall not be just a dilettante, but rather a free exerciser of their divine calling. To me during your lecture the doors to the revelation of John, which nobody can open and nobody can close[*], hovered before my eyes. You seem to be able to open and close them and are thus certain of entry to the sanctum." —

The Doctor replied, "The doors stand before us. We all, but each for himself alone, have our own doors and must be able to open and close them. Each has his own entrance into the temple of eternity, each also his own key. By that the Christian religion obtains universality, because everyone must learn to recognise it with their own powers. It lies in every human's heart: each may just seek in order to find, just knock and it shall be open to them, and each only ask in order to receive[†]. But you must knock within yourself, seek within yourself, ask in your inner-being. The source from which we can draw is in us alone; in us Christ must be resurrected as high priest in order to consecrate us for life. If we seek without, we will find nothing. What we do not discover within ourselves remains lost to us. In divine things no objectivity is to be found at all, no knowing takes place outside anymore. Here everything is subjective, we are ourselves everything, and hence each must be able to open and close the doors for themselves."

---

* [Tr.: cf. Revelations 3:7–8.]
† [Tr.: cf. Matthew 7:7.]

Reconciliation

One of the three parsons, by the name of Pfriener, who, since dedicating himself to theology, had adhered fearfully to dogma, responded.

Pfriener: "In this way the human possesses a freedom which must fill him with horror."

Doctor: "The human is unconditionally free. He can choose: life or death."

Pfriener: "Can he arrive at life without salvation?"

Doctor: "He must be saved through the rebirth, through Christ within him."

Pfriener: "What is the rebirth?"

Doctor: "The awakening of spiritual, that is, of prophetic powers in us."

Pfriener: "Is that possible?"

Doctor: "The examples contained in the Old and New Testaments of the Bible testify to it, thus we as Christians must not doubt in it."

Pfriener: "Then the human should not be able to sin."

Doctor: "The human must be able to sin, otherwise he is not free."

Pfriener: "Who brought sin into the world?"

Doctor: "If I say Satan or the serpent, then I mean by that the serpent which resides in our hearts, and there the freedom of the human is established again because he can obey the serpent or not obey it."

Pfriener: "But it would have been an easy thing for God to create humans without sin, that is, without Satan and without the serpent within themselves."

Doctor: "But then the human would not be free, would not have to choose, and would have to blindly obey the urges of the good."

Pfriener: "And would that not be considered the greatest happiness surely?"

Doctor: "No. The struggle makes one strong, victory brings reward. To us is prescribed life or death. We must choose, must struggle and thereby strengthen the powers of life. Were we drawn forcibly to the good, then I would have to compare it to a king's banquet from which we are not permitted to rise and must always partake. Here exists the freedom that we may rise from the banquet in order to create new hunger for ourselves; that we can choose the good, but can distance ourselves from evil. Anyone who seeks another freedom grasps for phantoms and becomes more of a slave, the more he thinks he obtains."

Pfriener: "If now a sinner met you, how would you convert him?"

Doctor: "I would bid him to go within himself."

Pfriener: "Provided that he did not do that, however, and did good acts instead?"

Doctor: "If he did good acts in order to avoid the effort of awakening himself, then all the good deeds would be of no use to him, to the contrary, they could for him turn into the temptation of justifying himself and hallowing himself in his deeds."

Pfriener: "Consequently are good deeds more dangerous than useful?"

Doctor: "Do not let the left know what the right gives[*]. Do the one without abandoning the other, these are natural laws. Anyone who has found themselves will choose the right path; someone who has not found themselves will constantly sway into error."

Pfriener: "But this freedom, this self-help contradicts the spirit of the Bible and Christian humility."

Doctor: "The Bible says: except a man be born again in spirit, he cannot enter the kingdom of God[†]. — Christ says: I came not to send peace, but a sword[‡]. There is struggle everywhere, obstacles everywhere in everyday life. Should the highest happiness be granted to us without effort? — Should we be forced to a happiness which we did not wish, did not seek, for which we have not struggled and fought for? Only the good obtained by yourself has worth. Only that which we acquire with effort do we know how to treasure, because we appraise every ware according to the price it cost us. Someone for whom the good falls in their lap by itself will gape at it indifferently like the fool who finds a sack full of gold dust, but does not know the worth of the gold and shakes it out, taking

---

[*]   [Tr.: cf. Matthew 6:3.]
[†]   [Tr.: cf. John 3:3, Matthew 18:3.]
[‡]   [Tr.: Matthew 10:34.]

the sack with him though in order to be able to use it in the future."

Pfriener: "What you say is good, but so novel that it seems to the novice as if he, without being able to swim, is being thrown into a river where he does not know whether he will find solid ground or death."

Doctor: "We find solid ground in the Biblical text: The kingdom of God cometh not with observation:* rather it is within your heart. Anyone who earnestly takes this to heart and writes it on the tablet of their heart and mind must, if he only strains his power of thought to some extent, understand my system with his own logic and find that nothing else is to be put forward here at all if you do not want to do violence to nature and reason. God created nature and humanity; he can thus have left nothing behind which did not agree with both and pointed humanity to other laws. — God built creation. But in order to glorify himself, he also had to have creatures who could comprehend his works. Thus arose humanity. But it is not what we see, hear, and feel around us which invites us to give thanks and prayer; no, the reason for it is that we possess with understanding and distinguishing feeling the capabilities of seeing, hearing, feeling, and finally marvelling and giving thanks full of holy emotion. Animals also see creation, but without a spiritual impression. To them it is a chaos in which nothing isolates itself but the objects of sensual needs. In humanity by contrast, there is the light of order, of the spirit of creation, of the creator, and hence we say with right that the human is an image of God because he bears within himself the plan of creation just as much as the creator."

The Physician called out here, as the Doctor fell silent, "That is enough. Anyone here who does not believe is a heathen and should first make himself worthy of receiving the Christian baptism. — Doctor, I admire you; but feel still too weak to imitate you. But what is not can still become. For the time being I place myself in your phalanx and will appear with you against anyone who wants to get too close to you."

Dean: "Even against me?"

---

* [Tr.: Luke 17:20.]

Physician: "Yes, even against you. Had I a nephew or a son, I would ask the Doctor to look after him and to lead him between the two cliffs of rationalism and mysticism with certain steps through to life."

Dean: "You are right. On my paths a young man cannot wander because he would abandon himself to the mockery of the world. — To investigate and comprehend our sacred matter with the spirit of rationalism is even according to the statements of the good Doctor himself not possible. In his system drawn from the Bible is a golden middle way where God and world are not so divorced as to not be able to give both what belongs to them. — I was not familiar with the Doctor's path, considered him to be a despiser of our sacred religion and was deeply concerned to know that my nephew was in his company. I have learnt otherwise and offer my hand to the one whom I was concerned about, and to the Doctor whom I misjudged, and ask him to drown everything which has occurred between us in the Lethe*."

"Splendid, splendid!", everybody called as one. The Physician took the Dean in his arms and said, "I knew surely that a good core is in him, and that is why I looked after him at every opportunity. But today he has delivered his masterpiece. — Long live our valiant Dean!"

Everybody repeated this toast; the Assessor, however, pressed his uncle's hand full of joy to his chest.

"Now bring out the champagne!", the Physician ordered — "the clergymen may see surely for once how laypeople enjoy themselves." — The champagne arrived. They drank and were joyful. The conversation turned general, everybody still had something to say and to discuss. But when the time came to go home, the Physician said, "The Doctor is staying with me. I have him now in my residence and will not let him go so soon." — Hardly had the Dean heard these words than he responded, "If the good Doctor is staying here, then he is my guest. I have to make up to him and cannot do it in any better way than if I host him at my table and let him sleep in my bed. With the Physician he does not have a host, for he abandons everything for the sake of his patients; with me you will

---

* [Tr.: river of Hades whose waters made the souls of the dead forget their lives.]

be well taken care of as if you were at home; thus the right to hospitality is mine." — The Doctor objected that he was not equipped with a change of clothes. — The Dean responded, "I will send my servant today with a small carriage to the city. The Assessor will be able to give him from your things what you need, and tomorrow, before you rise from the feathers, you shall be provided with everything. For tonight you can be content with linen, dressing gown, and all that you need from my supplies. You will live with me just as you like. This evening the Physician will dine with us, and thus we can then properly consolidate what you have said today. Thus that's that."

The three friends of the Doctor departed and marvelled at the Doctor's power of conquering hearts. — The Doctor, however, exercised on the Dean such an influence that the entire community, but mainly the clergymen of his deanship, felt it in the most beneficial way.

***

About the Author

Johann Baptist Krebs (1774–1851) was a renowned opera singer, director of operas, freemason, and esoteric writer who wrote under a number of pseudonyms (in particular, J. Kernning and J. Gneiding). He developed a form of letter mysticism composed of the concentrated thinking and feeling of letters through the parts of the body. This practice, also described in his book *Paths to Immortality Based on the Undeniable Powers of Human Nature* (available from this publisher), had its Biblical foundations described in depth in his student Karl Kolb's *The Rebirth, the Inner True Life, or How do Humans Become Blessed?* (also available from this publisher), and was further developed by Karl Weinfurter.

Other works by Johann Baptist Krebs published by K A Nitz

Paths to Immortality
Based on the Undeniable Powers
of Human Nature

The Missionaries
The Path to the Teaching Profession
of Christianity
(forthcoming)

www.ingramcontent.com/pod-product-compliance
Lightning Source LLC
Chambersburg PA
CBHW032049150426
43194CB00006B/465